YOUR BEST PATH FORWARD

A PRACTICAL GUIDE TO NAVIGATING SENIOR LIVING OPTIONS AND PLANNING

For Older Adults, Families, and Those Who Advise Them

Brad C. Breeding, CFP®

Find Your Best Path Forward:
A Practical Guide to Navigating Senior Living Options and Planning

Copyright © 2025 by Brad C. Breeding

All rights reserved. No part of this book may be reproduced in any form or by any electronic or mechanical means, including information storage and retrieval systems, without written permission from the publisher, except by a reviewer who may quote brief passages in a review.
Previously published as "What's the Deal with Retirement Communities?"

Printed in the United States of America
2025

The author specifically disclaims any responsibility for any liability, loss, or risk, personal or otherwise, which is incurred as a consequence, directly or indirectly, of the use and application of any of the contents in this book.

This book makes no financial recommendations to the reader and should not be viewed as a substitute for the need to review this topic with a trusted advisor, resource or expert.

Endorsements

"Perhaps the most thorough and current explanation of the topic. Easy to understand in simple-to-follow chapters. If you have aging parents, or are starting to think about your own future options, this is a great place to start."

Jesse Slome, Director
American Association for Long-Term Care Insurance

"Brad Breeding strikes the perfect balance between providing an exceptionally comprehensive overview of retirement communities and making the material accessible and easy to understand. Choosing a retirement community is one of the most financially and personally significant decisions you'll ever make, and you're fortunate to have such a thoughtful and trustworthy guide. Brad highlights the key factors and subtle variables that can deeply influence your long-term happiness and well-being – insights that truly deserve careful consideration."

Chris McLeod
Director (Retired) Osher Institute for Lifelong Learning (OLLI) at Duke University

"Brad has an exceptional gift for helping people make sense of one of life's most complicated and emotional decisions—where and how to live in the next chapter of life. He approaches this work with both heart and intellect, blending sound financial guidance with a deep understanding of what really matters to people as they age.

What I appreciate most about Your Best Path Forward: A Practical Guide to Navigating Senior Living Options and Planning is that it's grounded in reality, not sales talk. Brad genuinely wants readers to make confident, informed choices that align with their goals, values, and financial situation. He lays out the options clearly—especially when it comes to understanding Continuing Care Retirement Communities (CCRCs)—and helps readers ask the right questions.

I recommend this book to anyone beginning to explore retirement living options, as well as to adult children supporting their parents through the process. It's trustworthy, practical, and filled with the kind of insight that can only come from someone who truly cares."

Dr. Nikki Buckelew, Ph.D., CSHP, CSDC
Co-Founder and CEO- Seniors Real Estate Institute (SREI)

Five-Star Praise for Previous Editions

(Previously titled, "What's the Deal with Retirement Communities?")

Highly recommended

"Clear, knowledgeable, and gets right to the meat of the matter. These descriptions are why I love this book. The author has clearly done his research and understands the most important considerations required before making this life change. Highly recommended!"

The "textbook" for understanding senior housing options

"I have been working in senior housing for over 35 years and it continually amazes me how little the market knows about varied housing options available. Mr. Breeding has written the definitive textbook to educate people. His book is a tool I use to help people understand the differences in the types of housing offered."

Very good resource. Well-written in plain English

"Very good resource. Well-written in plain English. Excellent points to consider. A great overview of your options. Provides some good questions to ask yourself (or prospective residents). Highly recommended."

Excellent review of retirement communities!

"Breeding's book reviewing retirement communities is an important resource for anyone approaching or in retirement, and for families who are facing decisions about placing elder family members in a safe environment. He goes far beyond describing amenities, actually guiding the reader to match needs with options, including costs. His guide discusses what people should observe, what questions to ask, and what pitfalls to anticipate with contracts, etc. The information is well-researched, current, and easy to understand. A valuable resource for anyone thinking about retirement living options. I highly recommend it."

An excellent resource

"This concise book is filled with excellent information to guide you in researching retirement communities. It is extremely helpful in reminding the reader of the details to look for in each contract and important questions to ask prospective communities. Many statistics and averages are quoted, giving a solid foundation of what to look for in a community, whether in the financial, social, or nursing realm. Types of communities, financial assistance programs, and general phrases in this industry can be very confusing, and this book points out the differences so that the reader can go into the research process feeling informed and confident that they will be able to make an informed decision. This quick read is a great place to start when looking into retirement communities and will provide valuable information throughout the entire research process."

A must-read before you make a decision on any retirement living arrangement

"Easy to read and understand. Every option discussed without judgment. Good reference guide. Something every financial advisor and long-term care insurance agent should read!"

Very informative

"Comprehensive, yet simple and easy to understand. This book is a great resource for understanding the many options that are available."

Table of Contents

Preface	1
Introduction	7
1. I Just Want to Stay in My Home. Why Should I Consider a Retirement Community?	13
2. What Is a Retirement Community and How Can I Distinguish One Type from Another?	29
3. How is a Continuing Care Retirement Community Unique From Other Retirement Communities?	43
4. How Do I Make Sense of CCRC Residency Contract Options?	61
5. What Else Should I Know About Continuing Care Retirement Communities?	77
6. How Does Long-Term Care Impact My Retirement Housing Choice?	95
7. What are Other Ways of Paying for Long-Term Care or Funding a Move to a Retirement Community?	107
8. What Will Retirement Communities Look Like in the Future?	121
Conclusions	143
Resources	147
Works Cited	149
About the Author	157

Preface

In 2011, I was working as a personal financial advisor in Raleigh, North Carolina, when I received a call from a friend at the State Health Insurance Information Program for Seniors (SHIIP). He mentioned they were receiving a growing number of questions from older adults about continuing care retirement communities, also known as CCRCs or "life plan communities."

The problem? These people were seeking guidance on a complex and often confusing senior living option, but they lacked a knowledgeable and objective resource to turn to. This was particularly concerning given we were just emerging from the Great Recession, and many people were understandably hesitant to make major financial decisions.

At the time, I had never heard of a CCRC, but my friend at SHIIP also noted that many people asking these questions were highly educated and often financially well-positioned. As a young advisor, I saw an opportunity to pursue a potential niche: I could serve as an objective guide to older adults and families evaluating CCRCs while potentially growing my financial planning practice in the process.

I dove in headfirst. I devoured every article, book, disclosure statement, residency contract, and financial audit I could find on CCRCs. I even read actuarial reports ... voluntarily!

Prior to this extensive research, I, like many others, had considered most retirement communities to be "retirement homes"—places where frail "old people" went to live when they needed care. I never realized there were retirement communities that provided virtually everything a person may need for the rest of their lives, from vibrant, active living all the way through to 24-hour skilled nursing care—all on one campus.

With the blessing of the compliance department at my advisory firm, and in partnership with the founder of the firm where I was working at the time, we created a separate entity, which I named Carolina Continuing Care Consultants. I offered consultations for a flat or hourly fee to help families evaluate and compare CCRCs and related options. The initial feedback was overwhelmingly positive. The next step: launching a basic website and writing educational content on the topic, something few independent sources were doing at the time.

As luck would have it, a journalist from Kiplinger's magazine discovered our website while researching an article on CCRCs and contacted me for an interview. Without any PR push on my part, I was suddenly featured in a nationally recognized publication. Just like that, I became an "expert." Eventually, I would be interviewed by other popular outlets such as MONEY magazine, Wall Street Journal's MarketWatch, USA Today, and The New York Times. I even booked a few local speaking engagements—the first one was at a funeral home! As you might imagine, no one showed up, but other talks I gave were well attended. Before long, Duke University invited me to teach lifelong learning courses on CCRCs, and a major corporation asked me to speak to their employees about how to help their aging parents and other aging family members.

Word began to spread. I was amazed at how grateful people were to have someone knowledgeable to help them "figure all this stuff out." Many already had financial advisors, but few of those advisors had deep knowledge of CCRC contracts or pricing models. These advisory clients wanted to understand which senior living and care options made the most sense for their finances and other unique circumstances.

Thanks to my research and planning background, I was able to create the financial projections and scenario comparisons people needed to make confident, well-informed decisions. One challenge I encountered, however, was that most financial planning software does not incorporate the nuances of different types of CCRC financial contracts. This meant I often had to adjust or "work around" the inputs to produce reports that were as accurate and relevant as possible.

A turning point came one day while riding in the car with a friend who had recently exited a successful business. He suggested that my expertise, combined with independent profiles of CCRCs nationwide, could be packaged as a subscription product for financial advisors aiming to better serve their aging clients. He believed in the idea enough to offer seed funding to get the product off the ground.

After taking several months to weigh the idea and gather feedback from local and regional advisors, I eventually decided to take a leap of faith. Although I had a young family to support, I exited the financial planning business and went all-in on the concept. We hired a small team to gather the data and build out the reports, and the idea that would become myLifeSite was born.

Looking back, I didn't do nearly enough market research, especially on a national level. But the concept seemed to be very well received by most I spoke with, so I adopted the "life is too short" philosophy and went full steam ahead with product development.

Over the next year or two, I called on advisory firms all over the country, big and small. I even landed a few in-person meetings with some of the largest and most well-known brokerages in the industry, which was a bit surreal. Along the way, we expanded our product offering to include a robust resource library. We even developed our own proprietary financial projection software, which, unlike the other financial planning software programs I had used, is tailored to the complexities of senior living decisions.

But progress was slow. We found enough traction to stay motivated but not quite enough to scale quickly. Regulatory hurdles, compliance challenges, and data access limitations made growth difficult. After a year or so of modest success, with none of the anticipated "big deals" coming to fruition, I began to question whether this business could succeed—and whether my "life is short" mindset was a wise approach after all.

Then came another turning point: I received a call from a representative of a well-known senior living organization who had stumbled upon our website. He said he loved what we were doing and believed our unbiased written content and financial tools could be a powerful asset to his sales and marketing teams. His call was timely … and validating. It helped me realize that while I had focused initially on financial advisors, senior living providers themselves might be an even better fit for our products.

Soon, he signed up several of the communities he represented for subscriptions. From there, I hit the phones, cold-calling retirement communities across the country. The message resonated: Our online content and financial tools could help build trust, shorten the sales cycle, and ultimately empower consumers to make more informed, confident senior living decisions. Because when it comes to senior living, no one wants to be "sold." They want to be *informed*.

We began to gain further traction with senior living providers over the next few years. Although it was much slower than we originally hoped, we could at least see a path forward. In 2019, we launched a new proprietary planning tool called *MoneyGauge*^{TM}, designed to provide prospective residents with a simple, personalized report showing whether they are potentially a good financial fit for a particular retirement community. It quickly became one of our most popular offerings among senior living providers who want to equip their prospective residents with online decision-making tools they can use from home, on their own time.

Today, myLifeSite is primarily a business-to-business company, founded on the guiding principle of empowering older adults and their families to make informed decisions about their retirement living options. Moreover, we firmly believe the senior living industry benefits from a more educated consumer. From our weekly educational blog posts to our planning guides and educational videos, we strive to offer clear, objective information that demystifies the senior living landscape.

And that's why I'm writing this third edition of this book: to continue expanding on that important mission.

Originally titled, "What's the Deal with Retirement Communities?," I wrote the first edition of this book in 2014, a mere three years after I eagerly leaped into the world of senior living. I was surprised and pleased by the positive response I received to that original book release, as well as the second edition I released in 2017. It brings me great joy to know that the information provided in this book helps people make better informed, more confident decisions about their future. This is why I am equally excited about this third edition, now with a new title.

A lot has changed since I wrote the first version, but much is still the same within the industry. Based on what I have continued to learn through our continued research at myLifeSite, and through my conversations with consumers, industry representatives, financiers, consultants, and professional advisors, I have updated the book with new information and perspectives that speak to what I feel are some of the most important aspects you should understand about the changing senior living landscape, including an expanded description of emerging senior living alternatives, insights into the future of senior living, the history of CCRCs, options for funding senior living, and the potential tax consequences, as well as updated statistics and new charts to help convey various senior living pricing concepts.

Thank you for purchasing this book. I hope you gain as much from reading it as I have from writing it.

Introduction

In 1950, there were just over 12 million people age 65 and over in the United States, representing around 8% of the total U.S. population.[1] Fast-forward 60 years to the time of the 2010 census, and there were approximately 40 million people age 65-plus, representing about 13% of the total U.S. population.[2]

At that point, as baby boomers began turning 65 at the rate of 10,000 per day, the growth of this age cohort accelerated rapidly, expanding by another 40% over the next decade alone to reach 56 million, or roughly 16% of the U.S. population.[3] The pace of growth in the 65-plus population between 2010 and 2020 averaged about four times the annual growth rate seen over the previous six decades.

This trend is unlikely to slow down anytime soon. By 2040, the 65-plus population is projected to reach 80 million, making up nearly 22% of the total U.S. population.[4] To put this further into perspective, it is expected that within the next 10 years, for the first time in the United States, the number of people age 65 and over will surpass the number of people under the age of 18.[5]

Not only do older adults make up a much larger share of the population today, but they are also living significantly longer. In 1950, a 65-year-old could expect to live about 11 more years, on average. Today, most 65-year-olds can expect to live roughly another 18 years—an increase of about 60%.[6] And of course, many will live well beyond this average, but often not without chronic health conditions requiring some form of long-term care.

This rapid growth in the older adult population, combined with their longer average lifespans, has far-reaching societal implications, placing additional strain on our healthcare systems and federal programs such as Medicare, Medicaid, and Social Security, while simultaneously reshaping the labor force and economy. It also brings significant societal challenges, particularly in the availability of paid and family caregivers to support our aging population.

AARP prepared a study in 2013 analyzing the caregiver support ratio in the U.S., which measures the number of potential family caregivers age 45 to 64 for each person age 80 or greater.[7] At the time of the report, there were more than seven potential family caregivers for every person in the high-risk age group of 80-plus. However, the report projected that by 2030, the ratio will decline sharply to 4 to 1, and it is expected to fall to less than 3 to 1 by 2050—a time when nearly all baby boomers will be in the high-risk years of late life.[7] If this projection holds, it will represent a nearly 60% decline in the availability of family caregivers over those 37 years.

Adding further concern to the decline in both paid and family caregiver support is the fact that the number of "solo agers"—people who are growing older without support from a spouse/partner or adult children—is simultaneously increasing in the United States. Since the caregiver support ratio referenced previously only accounts for potential caregivers age 45 to 60, it does not include most spouses and significant others, who are often the first to bear caregiving responsibilities. Yet, the number of individuals age 80-plus who are solo agers is rapidly increasing. According to the Joint Center for Housing Studies of Harvard University, there were around 4.5

million people age 80 or over living alone in 2018. By the year 2028, this number is projected to jump to nearly 7 million and then to just over 10 million by 2038.[8]

These statistics raise an important question for our society. Where and how will older adults live and thrive? For far too long, our society has taken a mostly reactive approach to addressing the lifestyle and healthcare needs that we may face in the later years of life. All too often, individuals and families wait until a significant health event occurs before evaluating their options, shifting into crisis management mode without the resources, flexibility in schedule, physical ability, or emotional capacity to handle such a task. Yet, the above statistics make it startlingly clear that it's more important than ever before to plan for your future, especially for those living alone or without available family caregivers.

Making a plan

While the rate of aging differs from person to person, financial planners and other professional advisors often segment retirement planning into distinct phases. Recognizing that the entire concept of retirement is being redefined, with more people choosing to work beyond the traditional retirement age of 65, planners generally view the early years of retirement as a transitional phase, often lasting about five years after someone retires from their career. This period is marked by the need to reevaluate spending habits, adjust income strategies, and settle into a new daily routine. For many, it's also a time of rediscovery—figuring out what brings purpose, structure, and fulfillment now that work no longer defines their schedule or identity.

For a person in average to good health, the mid-retirement phase is commonly thought of as the period beginning around the early to mid-70s and lasting until the early 80s, or as long as the person remains able-bodied and high-functioning. Many individuals in this phase can live an independent and active lifestyle today, but this is likely to change as they age.

The late phase of retirement begins when a person's health has declined to the point of requiring daily living support with little chance of restoration. Statistics from the American Association for Long-Term Care Insurance reveal that nearly 70% of all long-term care insurance claims begin after age 80.[9] At this stage, the goal is that all the planning done during mid-retirement helps to make the transition as smooth and supportive as possible, ensuring a higher quality of life despite the potential for increasing care needs.

If you are approaching or in the mid-retirement phase, now is the time to plan for your later retirement years, while you are still active and able. Delaying important decisions about tomorrow's needs may leave you and your loved ones facing difficult and often costly situations in the future.

One of the more important and complex decisions to consider in this planning process is where to live. The home and environment in which you live during these retirement phases play a significantly larger role in planning than many people realize and will likely impact nearly every aspect of your life and overall well-being.

Purpose of this book

Beyond motivating you or your loved ones to start planning, the primary goal of this book is to provide clear, straightforward information on the various retirement housing options- including aging in place- while also exploring the key considerations, benefits, and potential challenges of each. It is designed as a launching point to begin the research process as you contemplate the best retirement housing choice for yourself or a loved one with the understanding that even where you live today can potentially shape your future. No single choice is right for every person, and the path that is ultimately best will depend on your own unique set of circumstances and preferences.

There are numerous terms and labels used within and outside the senior living industry to describe the various living options. In this book, I will categorize each type of retirement community and clarify much of the terminology. Still, I urge you not to get too caught up in specific labels because a single term may be used in different ways by different people or organizations. By helping you understand how various retirement living options work and what to look for, you can consider how those options align with your desires and objectives without focusing so much on the labels or terminology.

As you learn about the various retirement living choices, keep in mind that *paying for care* and *access to care* are separate issues. For instance, owning long-term care insurance or having a substantial level of savings and assets will help pay for care, but it does not address the other aspect of the issue: where and how your eventual care needs will be provided and the impact it could have on your overall health and well-being.

Remember: You cannot possibly plan for every contingency because it is impossible to know exactly what the future holds, but by understanding the options, considering the pros and cons of each, and having advance conversations with loved ones, medical professionals, senior living providers, and other professional advisors, you can minimize and possibly avoid many headaches (and heartaches) in the future.

CHAPTER 1

I Just Want to Stay in My Home. Why Should I Consider a Retirement Community?

Survey after survey reveals that most Americans want to remain in their homes as long as possible, often referred to as "aging in place." It is interesting, however, that surveys on this topic are usually given to people age 50 and over, or in some cases, 65 and over. I wonder, however, if the results would be different if these surveys were given only to those, let's say, age 75 or greater. As they progress into the mid-phase of their retirement years, people in this age group often realize that staying in their own homes may not be as desirable or practical as it previously seemed. This may also be why fewer people move to a retirement community before age 75. Furthermore, if everyone fully understood the range of retirement living choices available today, the surveys might show a greater willingness to move. Nonetheless, many people want to remain in their homes for entirely understandable reasons.

Since staying in the home is the obvious alternative to moving to a retirement community, I want to cover some important implications of this choice. This will provide you with a point of comparison against the various types of retirement communities described in the coming chapters. First, let's examine some of the primary reasons people wish to stay in their homes and the key considerations associated with each option.

Familiarity

As they say: "Home is where the heart is." Many people prefer to be in a familiar setting, surrounded by memories that create a strong emotional connection. Remaining in the home means staying close to the places they regularly visit and have become comfortable with over the years. Examples would be the barbershop or salon, grocery store, place of worship, favorite restaurants, and neighbors.

Depending on a person's personality, moving further away from these familiar spots may or may not present a problem. Some believe that change is a part of life and that new experiences are always welcome. For others, particularly those who do not adapt well to change, a move could mean less activity, fewer social interactions, and poorer overall health. My observation is that the longer people wait to make a move, the harder it becomes and the more likely they are to eventually face difficult and emotionally challenging decisions, such as those involving adult children or others.

Cost

Staying in one's home is often seen as the most affordable retirement living option, and it can be, particularly if the mortgage is paid off. However, that's increasingly less common. Among Americans age 65 to 79, 41% now carry a mortgage—nearly double the number from 20 years ago.[10]

Even without a mortgage payment, the savings associated with remaining in the current home may be less than they first appear once you factor in all the costs of home ownership. For example, it's estimated that annual home maintenance costs average anywhere from 1 to 4% of the home's value—likely at the lower end for a newer home and the higher end for an older home.[11] For a home valued at, let's say, $400,000, that would be $4,000 to $16,000 per year. This may include replacing or repairing items such as the roof, HVAC system, water heater, house siding, or driveway, among others.

In addition to home repairs and maintenance, the impact of property taxes should also be taken into account. With home values roughly doubling since 2010, property taxes now account for a significantly larger share of the cost of homeownership.[12] Using the same home value as above and applying the national average property tax rate of about 1% of the property value, annual property taxes would be another $3,500 per year. In some states, property tax rates top 2%.

One of the more overlooked expenses of staying in the home is the potential cost of modifications that may eventually be required to ensure long-term safety and practicality. On average, people who opt to remain in their home as they age spend $9,500 on home modifications, but some spend significantly more—sometimes into the six figures.[13] If you are considering aging in place, it's important to begin assessing the need for and cost of potential home modifications now so you can properly plan without the pressure to do it quickly and under duress because of an unexpected health event.

Lastly, aging in place often leads to the need for in-home care. Depending on how much care is required, the cost of in-home care can exceed the cost of living in an assisted living community or skilled nursing center. According to Genworth/CareScout's latest cost of care survey, the average monthly amount paid for a home health aide in the U.S. in 2025 is $6,292.[14] However, this is based on six hours of care per day. Some people will require less care, while others will need much more. If 24-hour care were needed, the monthly cost could be closer to $25,000. This doesn't include the potential cost to family caregivers, who often provide oversight and assistance as needed.

By comparison, the average monthly cost to live in an assisted living community or skilled nursing facility in the U.S. is around $5,300 and $8,600, respectively. (The average for a private room in a nursing facility is closer to $10,000.) Since these are national averages, the actual cost may be much higher, depending on the quality of the provider, location, services, competition, and more.

Maintaining independence

One of the popular reasons people cite for staying in the home is maintaining their independence. In fact, some people *equate* staying in their home with independence. However, over time, without proper planning, there is a risk of becoming less independent if one lives in the current home.

It's important to consider what "independence" means to you. For some, independence means physical independence: the ability to live day-to-day, without assisted services and support. Others equate independence to simply staying out of a nursing home, even if assistance with daily activities is needed. And yet for others, it is more about maintaining control over their schedule and decision-making.

Regardless of how you define it, the concept of independence in the home is often based on the unrealistic belief that nothing will change down the road, which eventually makes moving out of the home necessary. If the transition from full independence is gradual it can be easier to manage than an abrupt change that results in hospitalization and an unplanned loss of independence.

Another challenge with maintaining independence at home is the potential effects of social isolation and loneliness. According to the National Institute on Aging, social isolation and loneliness are major hindrances to good health, putting older adults at risk for high blood pressure, heart disease, obesity, a weakened immune system, anxiety, depression, cognitive decline, Alzheimer's disease, and even death.[15]

Of course, not everyone who ages in place will necessarily face social isolation and loneliness. It depends largely on their family, social, and support networks. Furthermore, some people are more naturally comfortable with solitude than others. But as we transition through the later stages of retirement and physical mobility becomes more limited, the risk of social isolation, inactivity, and loneliness increases.

Avoiding the hassle of moving

Let's face it: No one *likes* to go through the process of moving. Yet it only gets more difficult with age. Some older adults choose to stay in their homes simply because they do not want to deal with the hassle of moving and figuring out what to do with all their "stuff" that has accumulated over the years. Of course, *someone* will eventually have to deal with all the stuff. This responsibility is typically assumed by adult children or other family members when such individuals are available.

Yet, for those who proactively make a move earlier, many find it rather cathartic to live in a new and uncluttered space. This new sense of freedom from accumulated belongings and clutter allows one to embrace a fresh new chapter in life more fully.

For those who have more difficulty parting with some of their possessions, one helpful suggestion is to identify only those things that you need every day and put the rest in storage. Whatever does not get removed from storage within a year or two can be discarded. If you have adult children and grandchildren, you can let them take what they want; they will discard it later if necessary.

Another stumbling block many people have with downsizing is that their belongings represent more than just "stuff." Many items a person faces discarding or selling have a story associated with them. It may not be the item itself that is so important but rather the story behind the item. I attended a conference a couple of years ago where the keynote speaker was Matt Paxton, host of the show *Legacy List* and formerly from A&E's *Hoarders*. During his speech, he described that once someone shares the story behind an item, they are often more prepared to part with it. He then spoke about how much family members can learn about a parent or older relative through these stories, while sharing some touching examples.

Many real estate companies and retirement communities will contract with senior move managers who specialize in helping older adults downsize and even stage their homes for resale. One of the increasingly important staff positions in retirement communities is the "move-in coordinator," who assists with downsizing decisions, realtor and mover referrals, interior space planning for the new home, and moving day logistics.

Apprehension about 'living in community'

Although the health benefits of social connection and the sense of belonging that come from community living are well-documented, not everyone feels immediately comfortable with the idea of moving into a communal environment. For some, the hesitation stems from concerns about group dynamics, such as disagreements, incompatible personalities, community politics, social cliques, stigmas, or worries about maintaining personal privacy.

These considerations underscore the critical importance of a retirement community's culture. Every community has its own personality and values, and finding one that feels like a natural fit can make all the difference. That's why firsthand experience is so valuable. Spending time in the community—whether by attending events, sharing meals, or even arranging an overnight visit—provides an authentic glimpse into daily life. Whenever possible, doing so alongside current residents offers particularly helpful insight into how inclusive, supportive, and welcoming the environment really feels. It is also worth noting that even within a community setting, residents maintain the ability to decide how engaged—or how private—they wish to be.

The perceived 'finality' of moving

Some may resist the idea of moving from their home to a retirement community because they fear the perceived finality of the move. Even if life expectancy projections reveal the possibility of another 15 years or more, the thought of making what is perceived as "the final move" may be difficult for some to come to terms with.

Of course, it is important to weigh the pros and cons of moving now, under your own direction, and to a setting of your choosing, versus the chance of having to make a needs-based move later in life, likely with much less control over the decision-making process. The question isn't so much about whether your next move is your last one, but whether your next move—or even staying where you are—will help you live the safest and most purpose-filled life possible, while better preparing you for the potential changes to your health and mobility that may take place in the future.

Other considerations for staying in the home

Often easier in theory than in practice, aging at home can present many challenges, particularly during the "late phase" of retirement, which can sometimes be unexpected and cause a great deal of stress on families.

It should be noted once again, and as you will see in Chapter 8, that highly innovative technologies are being developed daily to help older Americans age more safely and comfortably in their homes, although it's still overwhelming for many homeowners of any age to use, manage, and maintain in-home technologies. Yet, there will always be certain obstacles associated with aging at home that are difficult to overcome with technology alone, not the least of which is the need for personal interaction. Although it is worth noting that in the next 10 to 15 years, some older adults may well have robots in their homes that resemble and respond much like humans!

Since it is impossible to predict exactly what healthcare needs and other challenges will arise in the future, it is essential to consider a range of scenarios if you choose to remain in your home as you age. These are some of the scenarios that should be thoughtfully considered in advance and discussed with family members:

- **Would your home need to be modified to accommodate potential mobility challenges?** The most obvious considerations include whether your bedroom and bathroom are upstairs or downstairs, and accessibility into the home. Other considerations include the width of doorways and hallways, as well as the height of the stove and cabinets, which are particularly important if you ever require a wheelchair. Other factors, such as poor lighting and hazardous flooring, can increase the risk of falls, a leading cause of admission to nursing homes. These considerations are part of the broader concept of "universal design," which focuses on creating products and living environments that are safe, accessible, and usable for people of all abilities and characteristics.

- **Who will maintain your home and property when daily physical activity becomes more challenging?** While this may be one of the easier challenges to plan for by hiring services, it's just one more thing to have to manage at a stage of life when it may be desirable to manage fewer rather than more things.

- **What will you do to maintain your sense of purpose and stay socially active?** Both of these remain essential throughout life to minimize loneliness and social isolation, particularly if your mobility and physical capabilities decline.

- **Who will provide transportation to doctors' appointments and other necessary errands if you are no longer able to drive safely?** At the time of the last edition of this book in 2017, ride-sharing companies had started developing ways to help older adults in this area. More recently, Uber has introduced a new service called Uber Health to support non-emergency medical transportation (NEMT), including preventive doctor's appointments, medication delivery, and other related services. Family caregivers can even schedule rides on behalf of a family member and track their trip status. This is a much-welcome transportation option, although not everyone is yet comfortable with it. Fully self-driving cars (Level 5 autonomy) may eventually provide significant assistance in this area, but the widespread adoption of these vehicles will likely take much longer than some had hoped or expected. Even innovative cities like San Francisco, which are usually on the forefront of technology, are showing less enthusiasm for self-driving cars until the technology evolves substantially. That said, Robo-taxis are expanding usage in some areas of the country and could play a bigger role in senior transportation within the next 10 years, if proven to be a safe and effective option.

- **What will you do to make sure someone is alerted if you fall and cannot get up on your own?** There are myriad technological solutions available on the market for this issue, but you will need to do the proper research to determine the best one for you and your family.
- **If your cognitive functionality begins to decline, who will manage your household and finances?** Someone will need to be on point to make sure your bills are paid, appointments are met, necessary services are provided, etc.
- **Will you rely on family members to help you prepare meals, get dressed, and perform other activities of daily living when you are no longer physically able?** It is essential to clearly discuss what your expectations of loved ones are in this scenario and get buy-in from those you plan to rely on.
- **If you require paid in-home care or assistance, who will manage the scheduling of caregivers and payments, as well as provide regular oversight to ensure that adequate care is provided and help prevent elder abuse?** It's also important to recognize that even with paid in-home care, a family member will usually need to be available to help fill gaps.
- **If you require facility-based rehab care following an unexpected injury, such as a fall, do you know the available options in your area and the quality of care provided by each?** You should have an idea of whether they generally have availability or what the wait list options are. You should also be clear on which ones accept Medicare and Medicaid (if necessary), and which ones are private pay.
- **Have you interviewed care coordinators and case management companies in case you or your loved ones need to draw upon the expertise of these professionals when assisted living or increased healthcare needs arise?** Having such conversations with these

providers well in advance of a need can help you and your family plan more effectively.
- **Do you have any present health conditions or illnesses that might become more difficult to manage in the future, such as diabetes or chronic lower respiratory diseases?** Such illnesses could present increased challenges as you seek to remain in your home.

In-home care options

As we'll further explore in Chapter 6, most senior adults will require at least some form of long-term care during their lifetime. Therefore, if you choose to stay in your own home, it is essential to be aware of the types of in-home caregiving services and supports available. Here is a brief explanation of the options:

Family caregivers

A family caregiver, also known as an "informal caregiver," is a relative or a close friend of an individual who requires some degree of assistance with daily living. They are usually not paid for their services, though some families may make compensation arrangements. Additionally, federal financial support may be available for caregivers when the recipient of care qualifies for Medicaid. [See more on Medicaid in Chapter 6.] In some cases, cash benefits also may be available for family caregivers through a long-term care insurance policy.

In 2021, the care provided by the millions of unpaid family caregivers across the U.S. was valued at $600 billion—a $130 billion increase in unpaid contributions from 2019.[16] Notably, this exceeds the entire amount spent on all paid healthcare in the U.S.

Although caring for an aging parent or loved one can be gratifying in many ways, studies show that it can also take a heavy toll physically, emotionally, and financially on the caregiver. Below are just a few statistics to help illustrate this point:

- Nearly 4 in 10 caregivers (39%) report they rarely or never feel relaxed.[17]
- Around 40% of caregivers who are caring for someone with dementia suffer from depression, compared to 5 to 17% of non-caregivers of similar ages.[18]
- Studies show that caregivers are 63% more likely to die from mental or emotional strain compared to non-caregivers.[19]
- Estimates show that between 40 and 70% of caregivers have clinically significant symptoms of depression, with approximately one quarter to one half of these caregivers meeting the diagnostic criteria for major depression.[20]
- Nearly 70% of caregivers report neglecting their own medical needs and missing medical appointments. [20]
- A MetLife study found that the average lost lifetime wages and benefits of a family caregiver is more than $300,000.[21] This study was done in 2012, so it's likely that the financial effects on caregivers are even greater today. And this doesn't account for the more than $7,000 per year on average that caregivers spend out of their own pocket on their care recipient.[22]

This last point above ties into the previous conversation about whether home care is a less expensive senior living route. While relying on the assistance of an unpaid family caregiver may directly reduce the cost to the care recipient, much of the burden of the cost may be transferred indirectly to the family caregiver in the form of lost wages and reduced future benefits, as well as possible out-of-pocket costs and medical costs associated with the mental, emotional, and physical toll of caregiving.

Home care services & home healthcare providers

While the terms are similar and often used interchangeably, a distinction can be made between "home care service providers" and "home healthcare providers."

Home care service providers deliver *non-medical* services in the home, specifically assistance with activities of daily living (ADLs) and instrumental activities of daily living (IADLs), which will be described in the next chapter. Some home care service providers are hired simply to provide companionship.

Home care service providers, sometimes referred to as "homemaker services," may not be required to be licensed by the state(s) in which they operate. However, if the provider also delivers home *healthcare* services, as described below, and accepts Medicare or Medicaid reimbursements for such care, then they would need to be properly certified with a Certificate of Need.

Home healthcare providers, on the other hand, deliver *medically oriented* care. Also known as "home health aides," providers of home healthcare are licensed by the state as licensed practical nurses (LPNs) or therapists and often work for home healthcare agencies, public healthcare departments, or hospitals.

Services delivered by home healthcare providers often include physical therapy, occupational therapy, and/or speech therapy. Skilled nursing care may also be provided, but typically only for short periods. Long-term skilled nursing may become challenging to deliver in a person's home. It can also be cost-prohibitive, especially if care is needed around the clock. In addition to skilled medical care, many home healthcare agencies also have staff available to provide non-medical home care services.

It is worth noting that the home healthcare industry continues to face a workforce shortage, exacerbated by COVID-19 and changes in immigration policy, making it sometimes difficult for consumers to find and retain quality caregivers. While COVID-19 increased the demand for in-home care, many workers became increasingly exhausted and frustrated with the compensation levels, which often fall within poverty-level ranges. Between 2020 and 2023, the home care workforce shrank, after more than doubling between 2010 and 2020.[23] Recent efforts to further tighten immigration enforcement are likely to worsen this shortage, as a significant portion of direct care workers in the U.S. are immigrants, and reduced entry pathways will limit the future labor pool.

The demand for in-home care is expected to continue increasing by more than 40% over the next 10 to 15 years, which will far exceed the availability of providers without drastic changes.[24] This shortage limits the ability of home care agencies to accept new cases and start care quickly. For families with immediate needs due to a sudden change in condition or an unexpected hospital stay, this presents a significant problem. The turnaround time from a physician or family referral to a home provider used to take a day or two. Now, it can sometimes take more than a week or two. In summary, while many people choose to remain in their homes for as long as possible, it's important to recognize that this may not always be the most practical, safe, healthy, or cost-effective option.

Housing decisions play a crucial role in a well-rounded retirement plan, and the decision to remain in one's home as long as possible requires considerable planning. Where you live can significantly influence your ability to support all dimensions of wellness—not just physical health and safety, but also your social, emotional, intellectual, vocational, and spiritual well-being.

When housing, health, or financial stability suffer, the effects often ripple outward, impacting not only an individual's well-being but also placing significant strain on loved ones who may be thrust into caregiving roles. Many caregivers simultaneously juggle their own families, careers, or both, making well-considered housing choices even more critical to alleviate these burdens.

CHAPTER 2

What Is a Retirement Community and How Can I Distinguish One Type from Another?

Retirement communities are not all created equal. The services offered and the extent to which they address the challenges that often arise during the "late phase" of retirement vary from one community to another. Yet, one characteristic that most traditional retirement communities have in common is a minimum age requirement, often referred to as "age-restricted" or "age-qualified" communities.

Although discrimination in housing is prohibited by the Federal Housing Administration (FHA), there is an exception for age. This allows for environments tailored to the needs of older adults while still complying with other FHA protections against discrimination based on race, religion, or disability.

The Housing for Older Persons Act of 1995 (HOPA) allows communities to restrict ownership to older individuals if either of the following requirements is met:

- All of the occupants of the community are age 62 or older, or
- At least 80% of the occupied units include at least one resident age 55 or older, and the community follows a policy that demonstrates intent to provide housing for those age 55 or older.

In addition to the above, the senior living provider must also demonstrate intent to provide housing for older adults, as reflected in its policies and procedures. Furthermore, the community must regularly verify and document the residents' ages.

The continuum of care

Aside from the more obvious characteristics, such as size of the community, amenities, culture, and location, one of the most important factors to consider when distinguishing one retirement community from another is which phase(s) along the continuum of care the community is equipped to serve.

Within the context of senior living, the term "continuum of care" refers to the increasing intensity of care services that may be required as a person ages—beginning with independent living and progressing to personal care, assisted living, and/or memory care, and then around-the-clock skilled nursing and rehab care.

It's important to understand that different retirement communities focus on one or several points along this continuum, while some retirement communities provide services spanning the entire continuum.

Here is an expanded description of each phase along the continuum of care:

Independent living

It is somewhat ironic that the first phase of the continuum of care is independent living, since this generally represents those who do not require much, if any, support or care on a daily basis. Independent living refers to individuals who are fully or mostly able to perform the normal activities of daily living (ADLs) without assistance from another person and do not require ongoing medical supervision.

Individuals in independent living may occasionally require assistance with household chores and other daily tasks. These tasks are sometimes referred to as "instrumental activities of daily living" (IADLs). New assistive technologies, including 24-hour safety monitoring and on-call services, combined with other traditional support devices such as walkers, wheelchairs, ramps, and rails, may help people to reside in independent living longer than in the past.

Assisted living

Sometimes referred to as "custodial care" or "supportive services," assisted living is generally considered *non-medical* supportive care and is designed for individuals who require assistance with one or more of the six main activities of daily living (ADLs): eating, bathing, dressing, toileting, transferring (walking), and continence. Medication management is also a core service that may accompany assistance with ADLs.

It's worth re-stating that assisted living focuses only on *non-medical* care. While recipients of assisted living services may not live fully independently, they do not require the level of 24-hour medical care typically offered in a skilled nursing facility (SNF, also known as a nursing home). That said, some assisted living communities are better equipped to serve residents with higher acuity needs and may even have nurses on site. However, with this level of assistance, the care provided falls just short of the types of services that would require a skilled nursing license.

Also worth noting: Assisted living services may be provided within a person's own home or in a community setting. Usually, assisted living services are first delivered in the home by a home-care service provider, often in coordination with a healthier spouse or other family member(s). Yet, as a higher level of assistance is required, some individuals and families may determine that moving to an assisted living community is the safest and most logical alternative.

Skilled nursing care

The Centers for Medicare & Medicaid Services (CMS) defines skilled nursing care as "nursing and therapy care that can only be safely and effectively performed by, or under the supervision of, professionals or technical personnel."[25] This type of care is prescribed to treat, manage, and monitor medical conditions and typically includes services such as wound care, intravenous (IV) medications, injections, rehabilitation therapies (physical, occupational, and/or speech), complex medication management, and nutritional counseling.

Skilled nursing care is delivered by licensed clinical professionals, including registered nurses (RNs), licensed practical or vocational nurses (LPNs/LVNs), and certified therapists. Care also is provided under the supervision of a physician and follows a specific plan of treatment.

These services are most commonly delivered in skilled nursing facilities (SNFs)—also known as nursing homes—which are licensed healthcare settings that offer 24-hour care. The quality of care in these facilities can vary and is often influenced by factors such as staffing levels, particularly the number of RN hours per resident and the availability of on-site physicians. Refer to Chapter 6 for further information on this topic. In some cases, skilled nursing services may also be delivered at home through licensed home health agencies when certain eligibility and safety requirements are met.

Memory care

In addition to what I have described above, memory care has become a common aspect of both assisted living and skilled care. Mainly focused on those with dementia, including Alzheimer's disease, memory care is usually offered in a facility setting, and the level of care increases as the severity of the illness progresses, often leading to full 24-hour care.

Today, almost all assisted living or skilled care providers offer some level of memory care services, although the level of service and delivery can vary significantly from one provider to another. Memory care often requires specialized licensing in addition to general assisted living or skilled nursing care, and the requirements vary by state.

Types of retirement communities

Now that you have a better understanding of the continuum of care, let's begin exploring the different types of retirement communities and where they fit along the continuum. The retirement communities covered in this chapter primarily focus on serving individuals who are either at the very beginning of the continuum of care (fully or mostly independent) or closer to the middle (with limited assisted living needs).

Each of the types of retirement communities described in this chapter falls under one of two categories: naturally occurring or purpose-built.

Naturally occurring

Naturally occurring retirement living options are not built by a developer but are instead based on a network of support within and among existing neighborhoods or through a virtual network of peer-to-peer support.

A growing number of neighborhoods are being classified as "naturally occurring retirement communities" (NORCs), which can evolve when residents of a particular neighborhood age together over time or when the neighborhood experiences a large influx of older residents.

The concept of a NORC was first defined in the early 1980s by Michael Hunt, then a professor of urban planning at the University of Wisconsin–Madison, and refers to any geographically defined community wherein 40% or more of the resident population is 60 years of age or older and lives in their own homes.[26]

NORCs are characterized by the emergence of organized entities to meet the needs of these older residents. They enable residents to remain in their homes for longer periods and adopt healthy aging behaviors by providing services tailored to their specific needs. In some instances, NORCs may be viewed more as a network of services than an actual community.

NORCs range in size and are often found in lower-income areas. No matter the location or resident demographics, the key to a successful NORC is identifying the unique needs of the community and providing the appropriate services to meet those needs.

Services and funding for NORCs are available through a combination of public and private partnerships, including contracted services, resident volunteer systems, social services programs, and community partnerships. The types of services available include, but are not limited to, social and medical services, case management, individual risk assessments and follow-up, transportation, help with daily activities, education programs, and more.

Some of the earliest NORCs emerged in the mid-1980s in high-rise apartment buildings around New York City. Originally created with private funding, the state of New York began offering government funding for NORCS and enacted its own NORC legislation in the mid-to-late 1990s. According to the Joint Center for Housing Studies at Harvard University, NORCs are most common today in metros in Florida, Arizona, and Oregon.[27]

Retirement villages (village-to-village networks)

Another variation of a naturally occurring retirement community, although it's technically not a true NORC, is a virtual retirement community. Sometimes referred to as "the village movement" or "village-to-village networks," virtual retirement villages tend to rely more heavily on peer-to-peer support and may expand beyond a single neighborhood to encompass larger geographical areas. Unlike NORCs, retirement villages are more often found among middle and upper-income populations.

As described in the report "A Tale of Two Community Initiatives for Promoting Aging in Place: Similarities and Differences in the National Implementation of NORC Programs and Villages," NORC and villages share the same general goal, yet they differ in how they seek to achieve it.[28] The village concept takes a more grassroots, neighbors-helping-neighbors approach to aging in place, whereas NORCs rely more on traditional health and social services, paid staff, and government funding. According to the report, members of villages are likely to be younger, more economically secure, and less functionally impaired than NORC program participants.

It is essential to note, however, that neither NORCs nor villages have on-site assisted living or skilled nursing facilities. Therefore, residents who eventually require care services beyond what can be safely or practically provided at home may need to relocate to a more suitable housing option within the community.

(For more information on NORCs and villages, see the Resources section at the back of this book.)

Purpose-built retirement communities

Although NORCs and the village concept are becoming more common, most retirement communities in the U.S. are "purpose-built," meaning they were designed and constructed from the beginning as age-qualified retirement communities.

Here is a description of each type of purpose-built retirement community:

Senior housing cooperatives

Senior housing cooperatives (also called co-ops) are an increasingly popular retirement housing choice for those who live independently. While the path to formation can vary, a distinguishing characteristic of a co-op is that it is usually formed and incorporated by the residents rather than by the developer. The development of the co-op may be resident-initiated, whereby a group forms a co-op to purchase a building or develop land, or it may be initiated by residents after they have purchased a building from the owner.

Co-ops offer maintenance-free living and other services, but are unique because the houses (including free-standing homes, townhomes, or apartments) and the land are owned by a "cooperative corporation," and the stock of the corporation is owned by the resident "members."

According to the Senior Cooperative Foundation website, "Cooperatively owned senior housing provides full apartment and townhouse living, controlled by the older adults themselves. All financial benefits accrue to the senior owners, including return of equity upon resale."[29] Just like with NORCs and villages, co-ops tend to reflect the mentality of their members as the sense of belonging and cooperation among residents is one of the key benefits of living in such a community.

When members purchase a share in a co-op, they acquire a stake in the corporation, which grants them exclusive rights to reside in a specific unit. The share price typically represents a percentage of the unit's value, which is based on several factors, including location, services, and size of the unit. The Senior Cooperative Foundation website states that this percentage is typically between 35% and 50% of the purchase price. The remainder of the cost and other operating expenses are covered under the residents' monthly service fee.

Pricing for co-ops is sometimes dictated by a practice called "limited appreciation," which seeks to limit the appreciation of the co-op stock's value. Although it may seem counterintuitive, the purpose of this practice is to help ensure a timelier resale of a resident's stock in the co-op when the resident needs to move. The concept is that units remain affordable over time, allowing waiting lists to build more easily, ultimately benefiting residents or heirs who wish to sell their ownership share. The cost of buying into a co-op that utilizes limited appreciation will also likely be more affordable than purchasing a home or paying an entry fee for a similarly sized home in another community. Timely resale is important because if a resident of a co-op moves out of the community, or following the death or a resident owner, the monthly service fee must be continually paid by the resident or their heirs until the unit is resold.

Co-ops are often financed using a "master mortgage," a single, overarching mortgage loan that covers multiple properties or units, which is insured by the state through the Department of Housing and Urban Development (HUD). Resident members pay monthly charges to cover their share of operating expenses for the community, as well as real estate taxes and debt service on their share of the master mortgage.

In effect, members of co-ops are their own landlords. Although resident members do not directly own real estate in a co-op, they are often still considered homeowners and may therefore be entitled to deduct from their income taxes their share of interest on the master mortgage.

Co-ops generally do not have healthcare facilities on site and do not directly provide any level of long-term care or skilled nursing care, although some continuing care retirement communities (described in Chapter 3) operate as co-ops. Therefore, co-op residents with advanced healthcare and long-term care needs may ultimately need to seek other housing arrangements.

Cohousing

Cohousing communities, also known as "intentional communities," could be considered a close cousin of co-ops. Cohousing has long been a popular option in countries like Denmark, Germany, and the Netherlands, but interest is increasing in the U.S., especially in areas focused on sustainability and community living.

From an outside perspective, cohousing may be indistinguishable from a co-op. However, cohousing communities are often structured as a homeowners' association (HOA) or condo association, whereby residents own their homes or condos directly and pay HOA dues rather than owning shares of a corporation. Alternatively, some cohousing communities may also be operated as a rental model.

More than any other type of retirement housing, cohousing residents often share a communal mindset. Unlike an actual commune, cohousing residents do not necessarily share a common economy or a particular set of beliefs; however, it is expected that residents will collaboratively plan and manage activities, share resources where practical, and support one another in various ways. This might include cooking meals, helping with landscaping for the neighborhood, or organizing resident activities and outings. In the context of this shared responsibility, residents who are less healthy and active may not always feel that they can contribute as much as they would like.

Another distinguishing characteristic of a cohousing arrangement is the presence of shared spaces. Shared space usually comes in the form of one building or a common house that is central to the neighborhood and includes things such as a kitchen and dining room for family-style meals, a recreational and fitness area, a laundry room, and more. The shared space is intended to help foster a sense of community and socialization. The common space may even have a few guest rooms available for visitors. The other side of this is that for some residents, cohousing may feel a little too intrusive when it comes to privacy and personal freedom.

It is worth noting that not all cohousing communities are age-restricted. Some cohousing neighborhoods have families of all ages, making them increasingly popular among people who desire the benefits of intergenerational living.

As with co-ops, cohousing communities likely aren't as conducive for residents who require advanced assisted living or 24-hour nursing care services.

Active adult neighborhoods

Active adult neighborhoods are planned developments designed specifically for active older adults who can live independently but seek a lower-maintenance lifestyle. Many active adult neighborhoods offer free-standing homes but may also include condominiums and townhomes, which are owned outright by the residents.

Some active adult neighborhoods are sprawling golf and tennis communities with a large clubhouse, for example, while others may offer more of a pocket neighborhood concept. Especially with the latter of these two, active adult communities are often developed near desirable local attractions such as shopping centers and parks, and some newer communities may even be located within a mixed-use development.

Homes within an active adult neighborhood are typically designed with features that are more favorable to older adults, such as smaller yards, a downstairs main bedroom, no-step showers, and more. Residents of active adult neighborhoods usually pay HOA dues for limited services, such as low-maintenance or maintenance-free exteriors, but are responsible for all other costs of maintaining their home. At other times, an active adult neighborhood may operate under a monthly rental model with a service package that includes amenities such as housekeeping, planned activities, utilities, laundry services, yard maintenance, and more.

Active adult apartments/senior apartments

As the name implies, active adult apartments and senior apartments are essentially apartment complexes designed for senior adults, offering various services and amenities. A distinguishing feature of active adult apartments, as with nearly all apartments, is that there is no central dining facility or meal program; residents are fully responsible for their meal planning.

Senior apartments, although similar to active adult apartments, tend to cater to residents with lower incomes. Some senior apartments are classified as "affordable senior housing," which qualify for HUD-supported government subsidies to help provide affordable rent or income-based rent. Active adult apartments, which are still quite affordable compared to some of the other senior living options covered in this book, often lean more towards a middle-market solution. (See more on affordable senior living in Chapter 8.) Additionally, unlike active adult apartments, senior apartments do sometimes provide dining services.

Lastly, both active adult apartments and senior apartments are usually not equipped or licensed to provide assisted living or healthcare services, although residents may contract with their own in-home care providers or those available through the community.

Independent living communities/rental retirement communities

Independent living communities—also commonly referred to as "rental retirement communities" or "independent living with services"—cater to those who seek to remain *comfortably independent*, delaying as long as possible the need to move to an off-site care facility.

Just like senior apartments and active adult apartments, independent living communities are rental-based. Therefore, residents do not purchase the unit or pay an entry fee, although there may be a smaller community fee due at the time of move-in. Compared to active adult apartments, independent living communities typically offer a more comprehensive range of services, including a central dining facility, expanded amenities, and sometimes access to on-site assisted living services.

At first glance, independent living communities may be confused with assisted living communities, especially as residents begin to age and require supportive services. However, the level of care provided and the overall number of residents receiving care in an independent living community is generally lower than what you would find at an assisted living community.

While some independent living communities hire their own staff or operate separate licensed assisted living units, it's more common for them to contract with an outside home care agency to provide services within a resident's apartment. These services tend to be more limited and intermittent than those offered in a dedicated assisted living community and are almost always paid for out of pocket by the resident. In some cases, residents may be permitted to hire a home care provider of their choice, although the provider may have to be approved by the community. Basic household services, such as housekeeping, which do not require licensing, are usually still provided by community staff.

Continuing care retirement communities (CCRCs)/life plan communities

Continuing care retirement communities, also known as CCRCs or "life plan communities," are unique from the other retirement living options I've described because they usually (but not always) provide services across the full continuum of care—ranging from independent living through assisted living, memory care, and skilled nursing care. Each of these levels along the continuum is typically available in one location, referred to as "on campus," and is outlined in a continuing care residency agreement. These agreements can take many different forms, particularly in terms of how residents pay for care services if and when needed. A deeper explanation of these agreements, along with the various financial models, important considerations, and other relevant details, is best reserved for the next chapter, which is dedicated entirely to this unique and nuanced senior living option.

CHAPTER 3

How is a Continuing Care Retirement Community Unique From Other Retirement Communities?

Continuing care retirement communities, or CCRCs, are a popular retirement housing choice among those who want to have a plan in place for their future. Over the past five to 10 years, the industry has increasingly used the label "life plan community" instead of CCRC, as it better resonates with the target market, emphasizing a crucial shift in the industry from passive care to more active living and planning. Yet, since most regulatory agencies still refer to them as continuing care retirement communities, that is the phrase I will use in this book.

The concept of a CCRC, first introduced about 130 years ago by faith-based and fraternal organizations, may be thought of as full-service retirement living because it provides a continuum of care- sometimes referred to as a continuum of living- typically spanning independent living, assisted living, memory care, and/or skilled nursing care, under a continuing care contract.

However, the specific types of care services available along the continuum can vary from one CCRC to the next.

Although average life expectancy in the U.S. decreased between 2019-2021, due in large part to COVID-19 and an increase in drug overdoses and accidental injury,[30] it began to rebound in 2023 and is expected over the long term to continue increasing as it has over the past 100-plus years. But with a longer lifetime comes additional concerns. Surveys of senior adults commonly reveal that some of the top concerns about aging and living longer include: serious health problems, being a burden on family, losing independence, running out of money to live comfortably, not being able to afford long-term care, safety and security, maintaining purpose in life, and having social needs met. For those who share these concerns, a continuing care retirement community may be a good solution. Yet choosing the right community is a significant and often complex decision, and it may not be a good financial fit for some retirees.

Many of today's CCRCs can be described as "high-end" or "luxurious," while others are a better match for the middle or upper-middle market. Lower-income or "affordable living" CCRCs exist but are not as prevalent and generally have fewer independent living residents. Where these exist, they are often operated by larger multi-site CCRC organizations that also offer more typically priced CCRC options. Like other affordable senior living options, lower-priced CCRCs are often HUD-financed and therefore only available to qualifying low-income older adults.

Varying definitions of 'continuing care'

As described further in Chapter 5, CCRCs are regulated at the state level, therefore different states may have different definitions of a CCRC. For example, my home state of North Carolina defines "continuing care" quite broadly as…" *the furnishing to an individual other than an individual related by blood, marriage, or adoption to the person furnishing the care, of lodging together with nursing services, medical services, or other health-related services, under a contract approved by the Department [of Insurance] in accordance with this Article effective for the life of the individual or for a period longer than one year."*[31]

To use another example, the state of Virginia has a similar but more narrow definition that includes the payment of an entry fee, written as *"... providing or committing to provide board, lodging, and nursing services to an individual, other than an individual related by blood or marriage, (i) pursuant to an agreement effective for the life of the individual or for a period in excess of one year, including mutually terminable contracts, and (ii) in consideration of the payment of an entrance fee. A contract shall be deemed to be one offering nursing services, irrespective of whether such services are provided under such contract, if nursing services are offered to the resident entering such contract either at the facility in question or pursuant to arrangements specifically offered to residents of the facility."*[32]

The state of California, on the other hand, has a much more nuanced definition of a "continuing care contract," which refers to *"... a continuing care promise made, in exchange for an entrance fee, the payment of periodic charges, or both types of payments. A continuing care contract may consist of one agreement or a series of agreements and other writings incorporated by reference."*[33]

It goes on to describe the continuing care promise as *"... expressed or implied by a provider to provide one or more elements of care to an elderly resident for the duration of his or her life or for a term in excess of one year. Any such promise or representation, whether part of a continuing care contract, other agreement, or series of agreements, or contained in any advertisement, brochure, or other material, either written or oral, is a continuing care promise."*

Given the variability in definitions of CCRCs, you will find that what one community is required to offer differs from another community, especially if each is in a different state. For example, some CCRCs do not directly provide skilled nursing care, instead offering advanced levels of assisted living and partnering with nearby skilled nursing facilities for rehab and skilled nursing care. Another example, as seen with the Virginia and California definitions, is that some states require the payment of an entry fee to meet the definition of "continuing care," while other states do not.

Beyond the state-level definitions of a CCRC or life plan community, there is also the matter of how various other websites and senior living organizations define such a community, which may be much broader than a state's definition. For example, if you go online to one of the more popular senior living search websites and select "CCRC" in your search criteria, you may also find independent living communities in your results.

Lastly, some states do not regulate CCRCs, and in those cases, there is no state-level definition at all. This doesn't mean that the care services provided by the CCRC are not properly licensed and regulated by the appropriate licensing body, but the state does not separately regulate the CCRC as an entity. For more on how CCRCs are regulated, see Chapter 5.

CCRC tax status

Upwards of 80% of continuing care retirement communities have nonprofit tax status.[34] Many are sponsored by faith-based organizations, although some nonprofit CCRCs are not aligned with any religious or charitable organization. And it's not uncommon for a non-profit CCRC to be managed by a separate for-profit management company.

Nonprofit CCRCs may operate independently as single-site communities or be part of larger organizations spanning multiple locations. In contrast, most for-profit CCRCs are owned by parent companies and typically manage multiple communities under a single corporate umbrella. Refer to Chapter 5 for further information on the distinctions between for-profit and nonprofit providers.

Over the past five to 10 years, a growing number of *for-profit* providers have entered the market largely because of favorable demographics and a growing need for senior living, combined with a favorable lending environment. More recently, however, interest rate increases, inflation, and historically high land valuations are making profitable CCRC development more challenging, especially for smaller organizations with less cash available to deploy. Higher-density properties with many units have become more favorable for development in the current economic and housing environment.

The appeal of a CCRC

Residents are typically drawn to CCRCs because of the unique combination of benefits they offer. These typically include:

- A wider array of services and amenities than most other retirement community options
- An emphasis on whole-person wellness and preventative care
- The reassurance of knowing that higher levels of healthcare will be available if needed—that full continuum of care that I previously discussed

On that last point, many residents describe their decision to move to a CCRC as a gift to their children or other loved ones, helping to ease the potential burden of future care decisions. CCRC residents tend to be proactive individuals who prefer to plan for their long-term housing and healthcare needs, rather than leaving these decisions to be made later by others. Often, the decision to move to a CCRC is made intentionally by the individual, rather than as a response to a sudden health crisis or family pressure.

Ideally, a move to a CCRC is the final housing decision a person will need to make, which can be a major advantage. Relocating becomes increasingly challenging with age—not just physically, but also mentally and emotionally. That said, as noted in Chapter 1, the idea of making a "last move" can be a psychological hurdle for some people, who may struggle with the finality the decision seems to represent.

In the previous edition of this book, there was a reference to a Newsweek article where the contributor summarized a series of interviews conducted with several residents of a CCRC in Maryland to gather insights into their experience. The residents expressed that they viewed the community as "a place to live and not a place to get ready to die."[35] Based on my own continued interactions with residents of CCRCs across the country, this is still a common refrain I hear.

Whether or not you choose to move to a CCRC, the lifestyle and healthcare challenges associated with aging must still be confronted eventually. The question is whether you want to live in a community that has services readily available to meet your needs when that time comes, or instead devise another plan on your own to address these potential needs.

To better understand how continuing care retirement communities differ from other retirement living choices, here are descriptions of a few key characteristics:

Contractual access to lifetime housing and care

In its truest form, a CCRC offers residents lifetime housing along with exclusive or priority access to assisted living, skilled nursing, and other health-related services, governed by a continuing care contract. This agreement—often referred to as a "residency and care contract"—outlines the services the community agrees to provide, the responsibilities of both the community and the resident, and the general framework for decision-making, including those related to care and residency. It also covers key details and stipulations related to monthly service fees and entry fees, where applicable.

> *Note: It's important to understand that some retirement communities offer all levels of care, like a CCRC, but do not offer a continuing care contract. They function as pure rental communities, where residents of independent living do not have priority access to assisted living or healthcare services. Residents may come and go from any section of the community at any time, provided there is availability. With these types of providers, each section within the community typically has a separate residency contract, and all residents pay the full market rate for care services.*

It's often said that CCRCs guarantee access to healthcare services, and in some cases, the residency and care agreements even use the word "guaranteed." However, more commonly, the contract language may read something like this: *"As a resident of the community, you are offered lifetime use of your residence and lifetime access to the healthcare center... You will be given priority access to the healthcare center over nonresidents."*

From a regulatory standpoint, there is typically no legal requirement for CCRCs to provide lifetime housing and care. In many states, the standard only requires that such services be available for a period longer than one year, but the intent and the way many CCRCs present their offering are often understood to imply a lifetime arrangement. And in practice, that's usually how it plays out: Most residents remain in the community for life, unless they choose to leave for unforeseen reasons.

Virtually all CCRCs also have contract language stating that if there is no availability in the healthcare center at the time you require such services, then the CCRC will coordinate arrangements with an alternate facility until space becomes available. Payment for the cost of care in an alternative facility will typically be handled per the type of residency contract. (See Chapter 4 for details on CCRC contract types.)

Prospective residents should ask a member of the CCRC's executive team to learn how the staff ensures space will be available for residents in the assisted living and skilled nursing care center, and how care coordination efforts are managed in situations where it's not. A well-managed CCRC will diligently assess the ongoing and potential near-term healthcare needs of residents, making it easier to plan for the necessary space in the healthcare center. If there is a glut in open healthcare units, many CCRCs will offer the space to others outside of the community to prevent the units from sitting empty. However, they likely wouldn't do so if they estimate an upcoming need for the space among their residents. On the other hand, some CCRCs do not permit direct entry into their healthcare centers, only allowing access to their continuing care residents.

If there is no space available in the healthcare center at the point in which it is needed by a resident, the community will typically do everything it can to help provide support to the resident in their independent living residence until space becomes available, unless it poses a clear safety risk to the resident or other residents.

When evaluating CCRCs, it's essential to understand not only whether assisted living, memory care, and skilled nursing are provided, but also the breadth of services available within these categories and how these services are delivered. For example, is memory care provided to residents in a separate section of the community or within the assisted living or nursing care center? What types of memory care services are provided, and are there any memory-related conditions that cannot be properly cared for at the community? What would be the alternatives in this case?

Entry and monthly fees

Although a growing number of CCRCs are offering rental agreements, the majority require an entry fee, which may range from under $100,000 to $1 million or more.

A CCRC utilizes the funds received from entry fees based on the type of residency contract and various other factors. In some cases, a portion of the entry fee is allocated to a healthcare reserve fund—effectively considered a prepayment of future healthcare services, which may help offset the future cost of care for residents. Some portion of the entry fee may also be set aside for long-term building maintenance costs and capital expenditures. Yet other parts of the entry fee may be used to pay down the community's outstanding debt and cover some of the operating costs. Lastly, some contracts state that if an entry fee refund is due to a resident or their heirs, it will be paid when their residence is either resold or reoccupied. As such, a sizable portion of some entry fees may be used to fulfill a refund that has come due. (See more on entry fee refunds in Chapter 4.)

Medical expense tax deductions

If any portion of the entry fee is determined to be a pre-payment of future healthcare costs, then that part of the fee *may* be tax-deductible by the resident as a healthcare expense. In some cases, this deduction can be quite significant. Likewise, a portion of the monthly fee may also be deductible, even while the resident is still living independently.

To understand how this works, it's necessary to first understand how the medical expense tax deduction works, which is potentially available to anyone, regardless of whether they live in a CCRC or not. As of 2025, if your qualifying medical expenses during the tax year exceed 7.5% of your adjusted gross income (AGI) and you itemize your tax return (instead of taking the standard deduction), you may be able to deduct that difference as a medical expense tax deduction.

So, what changes for residents of continuing care retirement communities? Let's say you move into an independent living residence within a CCRC. You are healthy overall and require no ongoing care services. Some people are surprised to learn that, even in this case, you may be able to take the medical expense deduction on a portion of the entry fee (in year it is paid) and the ongoing monthly fees. The reason for this, as described previously, is that a portion of your entry fee and monthly fee may be applied toward future medical expenses. Since this portion of the fee is considered a prepaid medical expense, it may be included in the formula for the medical expense deduction, along with your other medical expenses throughout the year.

For CCRC residents with a lifecare (Type A) residency contract or a modified (Type B) contract (each of which will be covered in more detail in Chapter 4), it is more common for a portion of the fees to be considered a prepaid healthcare expense. In rare circumstances, a smaller deduction may even be available for a fee-for-service contract (Type C), if it can be clearly shown by the organization that some part of the fee(s) is being used to subsidize any of the cost of care delivered by the community.

You should consult with your tax advisor as well as a representative of the community to determine if a deduction is available based on the community's financial model and your personal tax situation. Also, see the References section at the back of this book to find out where you can learn more.

Financial support

Many CCRCs offer financial support to residents who have exhausted their financial assets due to circumstances beyond their control. Of course, a resident cannot give all their money away and expect the CCRC to pick up the tab. However, if, for example, a resident requires substantial long-term care or nursing care services and depletes their financial resources, the CCRC may provide financial support to prevent the resident from having to leave the community. This is particularly true for nonprofit CCRCs, although some for-profit CCRCs also have separate funds or endowments available for the financial support of residents. While many CCRCs have a long and proud history of never asking a resident to leave due to the depletion of assets, it's important to know that this type of financial support will only be provided when funds are available and will not jeopardize the entity's overall financial position.

If the resident has a refundable entry fee contract (also described further in Chapter 4), the first level of financial support would likely be to advance the entry fee refund to cover the cost of care. If this does not cover the full cost, then all other available resources will be sought. For example, if the community is Medicaid-certified, then the resident likely will file for Medicaid first. However, many CCRCs do not accept Medicaid. In that case, the CCRC may tap into a financial support fund or endowment fund.

Financial evaluations

Prospective residents of CCRCs often must pass financial requirements before entry. In essence, this is a form of financial underwriting because a high turnover rate, caused by a lack of financial affordability, also presents a challenge to the CCRC model. Since the retirement community provides residents with priority access to a full continuum of care, often with discounted costs for care services, it's important that residents can pay the ongoing monthly service fee and any fees associated with healthcare services.

Furthermore, since many CCRCs offer financial support to residents facing financial hardship, it's important from a financial risk management standpoint to ensure the community is not over-exposed to providing this support.

On the other hand, if the community is overly stringent in its financial requirements, it may risk narrowing the pool of prospective residents too much, resulting in units sitting empty and lost revenue. This is a delicate balancing act, and the requirements could be tightened or loosened depending on the community's level of demand in the marketplace and its financial position at that time.

Many CCRC providers have an in-depth process for determining whether the prospective resident is a good financial fit for their community, including using sophisticated financial qualification software, but as a rule of thumb, they will generally look for personal assets equal to about one and a half to two times the entry fee, with a similar ratio for personal income compared to the monthly service fee. This is not an exact science as it does not take life expectancy into account, but it's a starting point.

Health evaluations

Prospective residents of a CCRC are also likely to undergo a required health evaluation, usually consisting of filling out a questionnaire and a cognitive assessment, and possibly submitting medical records. As you will learn in the next chapter, some CCRCs offer residency contracts that function similarly to a long-term care insurance policy, known as a lifecare contract. In this arrangement, a portion of the entry fee and/or the monthly service fee helps offset the cost of care that may be required in the future. Health evaluations are most often used by CCRCs offering these types of contracts because, under this model, it is particularly important to spread costs and risks across the entire resident population. Otherwise, it can put the community at financial risk.

For CCRCs offering a fee-for-service contract, where residents pay the market rate for needed care services, the requirement for health evaluations may not be as imperative. However, it can still help ensure that space will be available in the healthcare center for current residents who may need care soon, rather than accepting new residents who are also closer to requiring care.

Legal implications and restrictions regarding health evaluations

Some will debate whether CCRCs of any type have a legal basis for health screening to determine eligibility for acceptance under a CCRC contract. The guidance is not completely clear on this topic, in part because CCRCs offer independent living, which is subject to the Fair Housing Act, and assisted living and nursing care, which are subject to a distinct set of requirements under the Americans with Disabilities Act (ADA). But, for CCRCs offering a contract with healthcare services provided under an insurance-like arrangement, there seems to be a more logical argument for health screening.

In fact, almost all types of senior living providers have at least a basic health screening process to ensure that a prospective resident can meet the general "requirements of tenancy" and determine the appropriate level of care required. But laws require that all prospective residents be asked the same questions and that no one be singled out due to their appearance or disability. CCRCs should also ask only health questions relevant to the healthcare services offered, not those that might help the staff determine, for instance, if the resident will impact staffing needs.

It's important to note that using such a screening process to determine whether a resident will be *accepted* for occupancy is different than screening whether they can qualify for a continuing care contract. A CCRC should be well-versed in the fair housing and discrimination laws in this regard. For residents who do not meet the health requirements of a continuing care contract, the community may still be required to offer accommodation in the healthcare center at the market rate, if space is available, but there are exceptions. In some states, CCRCs with a certificate of need (CON) are required to maintain "sheltered beds" within the healthcare center that are designated for the exclusive use of residents and not the public.

An increased focus on wellness and active lifestyles

Virtually all retirement communities have a financial incentive to keep residents healthy for as long as possible. Several studies conducted over the years support the value of CCRCs investing in quality-of-life-related programming for their residents. For example, a joint study released in 2017 by the International Council on Active Aging (ICAA) and ProMatura Group showed a clear connection between so-called "wellness lifestyles" and customer satisfaction among residents.[36]

The study looked at the lifestyle/wellness data of 73 CCRCs in the U.S., as well as 26 other senior living communities that offer independent living, or both independent living and assisted living and/or memory care. Using customer satisfaction survey responses from over 3,400 residents of these 99 communities, the researchers examined topics such as the communities' activities, fitness opportunities, and recreation programming. They also tracked which specific wellness programs survey participants took part in.

This allowed them to make direct correlations about which programs offered the senior living community their biggest "bang for the buck" when it came to residents' overall satisfaction with the community.

Just a few key findings of the study that paint a very positive picture of the wellness aspects of CCRCs and the senior living industry:

- About 80% of survey respondents said that participating in their community's wellness programs made them "much more" or "somewhat more" satisfied with the overall community.
- Almost half of the survey participants said that they "agree" or "strongly agree" that the community's wellness program is one of the primary reasons they selected that community.
- Residents who participate in wellness programs live in the community for up to two years longer than non-participants, keeping occupancy levels high and reducing the cost of marketing empty units.

Most recently, the National Opinion Research Center (NORC) at the University of Chicago completed a four-part study funded by the National Investment Council (NIC) that focused on the health outcomes of individuals residing in all types of senior living communities.[37] Findings revealed that senior living residents:

- **Experience decreased vulnerability.** While older adults often become more vulnerable to adverse health outcomes before moving into senior housing, vulnerability levels off and declines shortly after moving in.
- **Receive more healthcare services at home (in the senior living community).** Older adults who move into senior living communities receive more healthcare services from care providers in their homes or apartments than those living in the broader

community. This includes more primary care services and more visits from specialty providers such as podiatrists, psychiatrists, and cardiologists.
- **Have increased longevity.** Older adults who move into senior living have a lower mortality rate than older adults who live in the broader community. They also receive more home healthcare days, obtain more days of home-based preventative and rehabilitative services, and are less dependent on antipsychotics.
- **Experience better health outcomes.** Older adults who move into senior living experience lower rates of inpatient hospital admissions despite higher utilization of the emergency department.

Each of the above is described in greater detail and broken out by type of senior living in individual reports available on the NIC website.

Comprehensive health and wellness programs at CCRCs may include access to qualified fitness professionals, special diet meal plans, aquatic and fitness centers, low-impact aerobics, and yoga classes.

Over the past few years, wellness programs have expanded far beyond just physical fitness, however. CCRCs today emphasize the "whole person" concept, including social, emotional, spiritual, intellectual, and vocational experiences and support, much of which is being further supported by innovative technologies and resident engagement applications. (Refer to Chapter 8 for more information on holistic wellness programming and its role in the future of senior living.)

The overall objective of nearly every CCRC is to foster an environment and provide options that allow older adults to experience a purpose-filled, creative, and satisfying aging process. This also includes several communal areas on-site for socialization and activities, as well as amenities like auditoriums and theaters, ballrooms for parties and celebrations, game rooms, woodworking shops, pickleball courts, cafes and bistros, walking trails, resident gardens, and libraries, among others. On-site lifelong learning programs and easy access to the broader community through service programs and university partnerships are also becoming increasingly common.

CHAPTER 4

How Do I Make Sense of CCRC Residency Contract Options?

When considering a continuing care retirement community (CCRC or "life plan community"), it is important to understand the type of residency contract offered, as there are usually trade-offs between what you pay now and what you will pay later if you require advanced long-term care or healthcare services. Often, a CCRC may offer several different residency contracts from which to choose.

Most contracts offered by CCRCs fall under one of five major types as described in the chart below:

Entry Fee Models				
LIFECARE (Type A)	**MODIFIED (Type B)**	**FEE FOR SERVICE (Type C)**	**RENTAL (Type D)**	**EQUITY (Type E)**
Pre-pay for unlimited care	Pre-pay for some care	Little or no pre-pay for care	No entry fee (maybe smaller "community fee")	No entry fee; home is purchased
Cost of care included in monthly rate*	Care services offered at a discounted rate**	Full cost of care services paid by the resident	Higher monthly fees, all other things being equal	If a co-op, resident purchases shares in a corporation
Predictable monthly expenses, makes planning easier	Discount may come in the form of "free days" in healthcare	Less predictability of long-term care expenses	Full cost of care services paid by resident	Monthly service fees or "membership" fees still apply
CCRC absorbs more risk for the cost of care	CCRC and resident share the risk of healthcare cost	Resident absorbs the cost of care, only pays for care needed	Resident may not have priority access to care services	Full cost of care typically paid by the resident

* Inflationary increases and ancillary expenses may still apply
** The discount may be in the form of a percentage decrease off the market rate, or a designated # of days in the healthcare center at no additional cost

In theory, if one CCRC offers multiple contract types, each one should be actuarially equivalent. *All other things being equal*, one type of contract should not be more advantageous than the other over the long term if the contracts are priced appropriately and use all the same statistical, financial, and actuarial assumptions. Yet, different communities may use different methods to "price" their contracts, so when comparing contracts offered by different CCRCs, this theory will not always hold true.

Whether one contract is financially better for a resident over the long term ultimately depends mainly on how much care is needed and for how long. Furthermore, other factors come into play when comparing pricing at different communities, including location, cost of living, lavishness, and more.

The first three contract types shown in the chart above require the resident to pay a one-time entry fee in addition to the regular monthly service fee. The concept of the entry fee model traces back to the earliest CCRCs. As mentioned in the previous chapter, the general concept of a continuing care retirement community first emerged in the United States in the early 1920s, although it wasn't until the 1960s that it began to experience rapid growth.

According to the book "Continuing Care Retirement Communities: An Empirical, Financial, and Legal Analysis," written in 1984 by Howard E. Winklevoss and Alton Alwyn V. Powell, the earliest providers of these communities were churches who felt it was their responsibility to offer housing and healthcare for their aging ministers and missionaries.[38] Over time, the appeal of this model grew among the broader church population.

Entry fees—then referred to as "accommodation" and "lifecare" fees—were central to these early CCRC models. The first continuing care retirement communities were funded entirely by turning over one's assets to the church, which, in some cases, was not enough to fully cover the lifetime costs for the individual and needed to be supplemented by the organization's endowment. It wasn't until later that monthly fees were introduced after providers realized that funding CCRCs entirely through the assignment of assets was often either insufficient over the long term or unfair to those with more assets than others. Eventually, the industry shifted from requiring a resident to assign their assets to the senior living provider to adopting an entry fee model.

Although there are a growing number of rental and equity (ownership) CCRCs today, the majority still operate under an entry fee model. Yet, the contract with the highest cost today, including both the entry fee and the monthly service fees, is not necessarily the one that will cost the most over your lifetime. The lifetime cost will depend mainly on the amount of care you require and what you pay for it, which is in turn based on the type of CCRC contract you have. Of course, no one knows how much care they will eventually need. If they did, planning would sure be a lot easier!

Here are a few additional details about the contract types shown in the chart above:

Lifecare contracts (Type A)

A true lifecare contract, also called a Type A contract, is a representation of the original CCRC model and may be thought of as an all-inclusive approach to housing and healthcare. All other things being equal (i.e., location, unit size, amenities, etc.), the monthly service fee and/or the entry fee should be higher for a life care contract than for a modified or fee-for-service contract.

The tradeoff is that although more is paid in the early years, a resident's monthly fees will not increase for care services provided in the assisted living or healthcare center, regardless of the level of care required. In this way, a lifecare contract works somewhat like an unlimited long-term care insurance policy.

This does not mean the monthly service fees will *never* increase under a lifecare contract, however. As with any type of retirement community, monthly service fees are likely to increase annually to reflect the impact of inflation on the provider's operating budget. Moreover, residents with a lifecare contract typically begin paying for the cost of either one or two additional meals when they transition from independent living to the healthcare center. Yet under a true lifecare contract, residents will not pay more for assisted living or skilled nursing provided in the healthcare center. The exception may be if a resident chooses to hire in-home care while still living in their independent living residence.

The most significant advantage of a lifecare contract is the predictability of lifetime costs for housing and care-related services. CCRC residents with a lifecare contract know that most of their monthly expenses during their lifetime will be covered under the monthly service fee, regardless of how much care is ultimately required or for how long. This simplifies the financial planning process by removing some of the less predictable costs associated with life's "what ifs." The flip side of this is that residents are paying more in the early years for care that may or may not be required in the future.

People often wonder how a lifecare contract works in the case of a couple. In this situation, there will be a first-person monthly service fee and a smaller second-person monthly fee. The two combined fees represent the double-occupancy rate. As long as both residents are living within the CCRC—regardless of where either person resides within the community—they will continue to pay the double-occupancy monthly rate.

Again, keep in mind that the leveled pricing associated with lifecare typically applies only when the resident is receiving care within the community's assisted living or healthcare center, not when a resident chooses to hire in-home care.

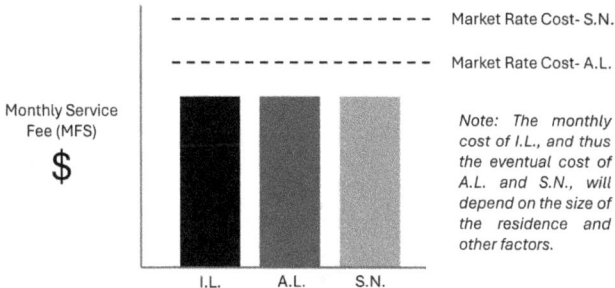

The above graphic illustrates the concept of a **Lifecare (Type A)** contract. The bars represent independent living (I.L.), assisted living (A.L.) and skilled nursing (S.N.).

Equalized-rate lifecare contracts

A newer version of the lifecare contract is commonly referred to in the industry as "equalized-rate pricing." With this type of pricing structure, when a resident makes a permanent transfer to assisted living or skilled nursing care, they do not necessarily continue to pay the same monthly rate they paid in independent living. Instead, they begin paying a pre-determined amount that is typically equal to the pricing for a specific residential unit.

For instance, the contract may state, "When a resident transfers to our healthcare center, they will begin paying a monthly rate equal to the then-current rate for our smallest two-bedroom apartment." This means that a resident in a lower-priced (typically smaller) residence would pay more for assisted living or skilled nursing care services, while someone in a higher-priced residence (typically larger) would pay less.

In short, an equalized-rate approach to lifecare could result in a resident paying a higher *or* lower amount for care services, relative to the cost of their independent living residence. The effect of this model is that it equalizes the cost of care for all residents, regardless of what they were paying while living independently.

It is important to note that in the case of couples, the equalized-rate for care will likely apply to each resident separately as they move, whether one or both move into assisted living or skilled nursing care. This is different from a true lifecare contract, where the couple continues paying the double-occupancy rate all along.

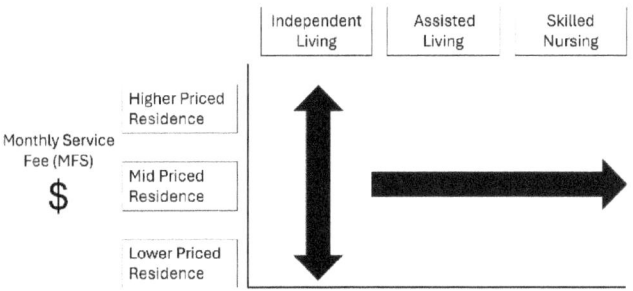

The above graphic illustrates the concept of an **Equalized Rate Lifecare** contract. The bars represent independent living (I.L.), assisted living (A.L.) and skilled nursing (S.N.)

Modified contracts (Type B)

Modified contracts, also known as Type B contracts, are essentially hybrid contracts and are not entirely different from equalized-rate lifecare. The entry fee and monthly service fee will cover the cost of some care, but not on an unlimited basis as a lifecare contract does. The typical discount may be anywhere from 10 to 20% or more of the community's market rate for care services.

In other cases, a resident will still pay the full market rate for care, but the contract allows for a certain number of prepaid days in the healthcare center. These "free days,' as they are sometimes called, may be offered on a per-year basis or over the life of the contract. The resident will continue paying the monthly service fee for their independent living residence, but care services are available at no additional cost during this time.

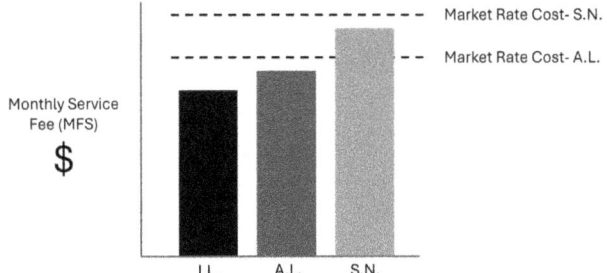

The above graphic illustrates the concept of a **Modified (Type B)** contract. The bars represent independent living (I.L.), assisted living (A.L.) and skilled nursing (S.N.)

Fee-for-service contracts (Type C)

In contrast to a lifecare contract, a fee-for-service or Type C contract requires a lower monthly service fee and/or lower entry fee, but in exchange, the resident will pay the full market rate for any care services provided by the community. Unless the resident was previously living in one of the most expensive independent living residences, this could mean an increase of thousands of dollars per month.

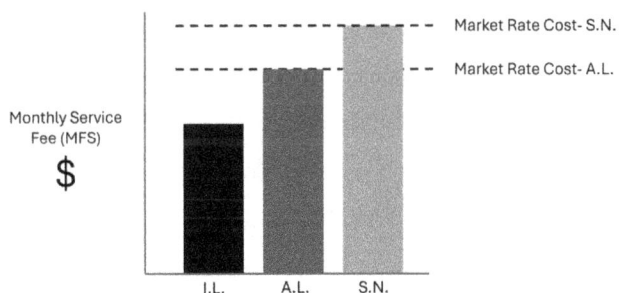

The above graphic illustrates the concept of a **Fee for Service (Type C)** contract. The bars represent independent living (I.L.), assisted living (A.L.) and skilled nursing (S.N.)

In summary, most residents with a fee-for-service contract will pay less while living independently, but substantially more if they require advanced care. The tradeoff is that they will only pay for the care they use.

With both a fee-for-service contract and a modified contract, it's especially important to consider how it works for a couple. Just like any other type of contract, the couple will pay a double-occupancy rate while residing in independent living, which consists of a first-person monthly fee and a smaller second-person monthly fee. If either person needs to make a permanent move to the assisted living or healthcare center, the person remaining in independent living will only pay the first person (single occupancy) fee, while the other person will begin paying for the higher cost of care services. Later, if the person who previously remained in independent living also makes a permanent move to the assisted living or healthcare center, the single occupancy rate for independent living will then drop off and that person will begin paying the full cost of care as well. If both people are receiving care at the same time, they would both pay the full combined cost of care. However, if they are sharing a unit in the care center, the total cost may be lower.

One last note on this matter: Most CCRC contracts delineate between a *temporary* transfer to the healthcare center and one that is deemed *permanent*. In the case of a temporary transfer by either person, the double-occupancy rate will typically still be charged while the person is paying for care. Thus, in this situation, the cost of care for the temporary time period may be charged *in addition to* the independent living monthly fees. Keep in mind that what I've described applies to fee-for-service and modified contracts, as well as equalized-rate lifecare in some cases. A true lifecare contract works differently in this situation for couples, as described previously.

Rental contracts (Type D)

For people who like the idea of access to a continuum of care but do not want to pay an entry fee, a rental contract (also called a Type D contract) might make sense. *All other things being equal*, the monthly service fee for a rental CCRC contract will be higher from day one than it would be for any of the other types of contracts. Afterall, the money must come from somewhere.

Keep in mind, as described previously, some rental communities may offer a full continuum of care without offering a continuing care agreement. Therefore, residents do not have priority access to the care services under a continuing care agreement and don't benefit from some of the other unique characteristics of a CCRC.

Just like with a fee-for-service contract, residents with rental contracts will pay the then-current market rate for care when services are received in the healthcare center. In the case of a couple, the fee adjustments that occur when one or both residents require care would function the same way as I described for fee-for-service and modified contracts.

Equity/co-op contracts (Type E)

Residents in equity CCRCs own their homes or apartments. However, they are still required to pay a monthly service fee, sometimes referred to as a "membership fee," for services and amenities, including home maintenance. Some CCRCs operate under the co-op model, described in Chapter 2, whereby residents purchase shares of the corporation. Under both arrangements, healthcare services are usually offered at the full market rate or at a slight discount.

Under a true equity model, the resident owns their home or condo outright, and it will eventually pass on to the resident's heirs or the estate, just as any home would. One important consideration, however, is that the monthly service fee may continue until the heirs resell the residence to another person who qualifies based on age, finances, and health.

It should also be noted that some equity CCRC models are not a true ownership arrangement. Rather, if a resident moves out of the community or passes away, the operator still owns and resells the residence, but the resident, or the resident's heirs, receives a predetermined portion of any price appreciation realized during the sale.

Refundable entry fees

Entry fees at CCRCs are almost always refundable, up to a certain point. Traditional contracts are usually "declining balance" contracts, meaning the entry fee will be refundable to a resident or their heirs on a declining basis over the first few years of residency, after which the resident will not receive any portion of their entry fee back. A refundable contract, also known as a "return of capital" plan, is refundable in part or in full, regardless of the amount of time that has elapsed. Common refundable contracts are 50%, 75%, and 90%.

Here are a couple of examples of how entry-fee refund options work:

Declining balance entry fee contract

The entry fee for a two-bedroom cottage at ABC Community is $290,000. Under the traditional contract, the community gets 4% of the entry fee upfront, and then it amortizes at 2% each month for the next 48 months, totaling 100%. [4% + (2% x 48 months) = 100%] If, for instance, the resident moves out of the CCRC or passes away in the 36th month, then 76% of the entry fee, or $220,400, stays with the community [4% + (2% x36 months) = 76%]. The remaining 24%, or $69,600, would go to the resident or the resident's heirs. If the resident is still living in the community after four years, no refund will be available from that point forward.

Refundable entry fee contract

ABC Community also offers a 50% refundable contract. If the resident elects this option, the entry fee for the same home or apartment used in the example above is now $380,000—an increase of about 31% over the traditional contract fee. In this case, the community still amortizes 4% of the entry fee up-front and then 2% per month for the next 23 months, as opposed to 48 months in the prior example. This is a total of 50% that is retained by the community [4% + (2% x 23 months) = 50%]. After two years, the community does not further amortize any of the entry fee, so the resident or their heirs receive the full 50% refund. In this example, the resident, or the resident's estate, will receive back a minimum of $190,000 [50% x $380,000] no matter how long the resident lives in the community, and possibly more if the occurrence takes place within the first two years.

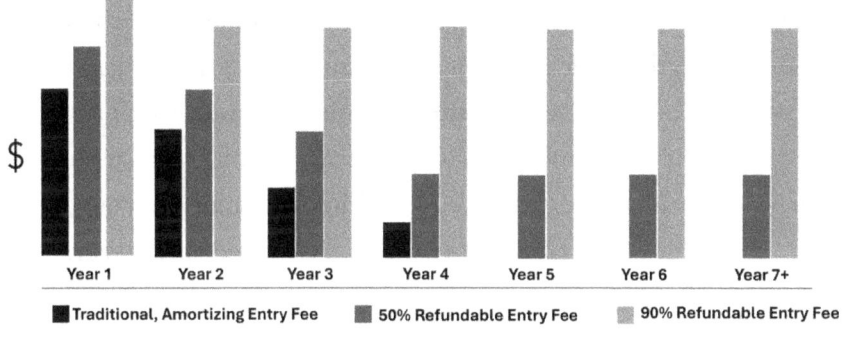

The above graphic illustrates three types of CCRC entry fee refunds. There are other options available among CCRCs which not illustrated here.

Entry fee refund stipulations

Prospective residents considering a refundable entry fee contract should clearly understand the contract's stipulations for receiving a refund. For instance, does a new entry fee need to be received on the same unit before the entry fee refund is paid? Does the unit have to be reoccupied before it is paid? Is there a maximum time limit for refund payment, regardless of whether a new entry fee is received or the unit is reoccupied? And is there a priority order in which residents or their heirs receive refunds? These are just a few examples of the types of stipulations that are important to understand and should be covered in the residency agreement.

Although it's not common, some entry-fee CCRCs will require residents or their heirs to continue paying the monthly fee until the unit is reoccupied. Again, this is more commonly seen with equity (Type E) contracts. This provision is a double-edged sword. It helps provide financial stability for the community by ensuring that, for financial purposes, there are no vacant units on site. However, it is not always viewed favorably by the resident or the resident's heirs, who must bear the burden of the payments until re-occupancy.

You should also ask if the community sets aside a portion of the entry fees in a reserve account to help fulfill future entry fee refunds. If the community relies entirely on the resale of the unit to pay the refund, the resident or their heirs could risk not receiving the refund promptly. It usually isn't a problem if demand for the community is high and there is a strong waitlist. However, this may not always be the case, especially if the community falls out of favor or an economic downturn occurs. As mentioned previously, some communities have a maximum time limit, described in their contract, within which the entry fee refund is to be paid. Some states even require such a provision for CCRCs.

For example, the State of California enacted legislation in 2016 differentiating between *repayable* and *refundable* contracts, with refundable contracts requiring more stringent reserve requirements. Repayable agreements depend on the resale of the unit but not necessarily the specific unit in which the resident previously resided. Instead, residents who are due repayment are entered into a larger pool and refunds are paid in sequential order as entry payments are received from new residents. However, if the repayment amount is not fully paid within 180 days after the unit is permanently vacated then 4% interest applies to the balance until the lump sum is paid. After 240 days, the interest on the unpaid balance increases to 6%.

Other states, such as New Jersey and Connecticut, have passed similar legislation stipulating a maximum time frame within which entry fee refunds must be paid. Even without state regulatory requirements, some CCRC providers choose to enact maximum time limits on entry fee refunds or repayments.

Continuing care at home (CCAH)

In addition to the contract types described above, continuing care at home (CCAH) is an increasingly popular program being offered by some CCRCs. CCAH extends in-home services and care to "members"—people who may later become full-time residents of the community. Often referred to as a "CCRC without walls," this model is likely to continue growing as CCRCs seek to attract more older adults who want to stay at home for as long as possible, but who appreciate the concept of priority access to care at a predictable price.

A CCAH contract provides access to the same continuum of care, as well as many of the other services offered by the CCRC. However, instead of moving into the community, a CCAH member remains in their own home until they are ready, although moving into the community is not a requirement. As with traditional CCRCs, members of a CCAH program must be generally healthy to enter into a contract.

Importantly, a CCAH contract differs from simply purchasing in-home care or support services on an as-needed basis. In the report *CCRC Without Walls: Care Models of the Future*, Stephen Maag, former director of residential communities at LeadingAge, explains that what sets a CCRC without walls apart is its ability to bring the core elements of a lifecare contract- including a coordinated package of services- directly into a person's current home. Rather than offering individual services on an as-needed basis, this model provides a more integrated and proactive approach to supporting the health and wellness of older adults as they age in place.[39]

While many CCAH programs are affiliated with traditional continuing care retirement communities, some operate independently, partnering with local providers rather than being tied to a physical campus. That said, affiliation with a CCRC can offer notable advantages, such as priority access to on-site care if a participant eventually needs it, or chooses to transition out of the home. Additionally, members of affiliated programs often benefit from access to on-campus amenities while still receiving a bundled package of services in their own homes. These typically include care coordination, transportation, in-home nursing, and assistance with household chores and errands.

Indeed, the success of a CCAH program depends largely on the availability of reliable care coordination. Members are typically assigned a dedicated care coordinator or a service facilitator, who will conduct an orientation meeting with new members. This helps the coordinator to know members personally and to hopefully build a trusting relationship. The care coordinator will become the member's advocate when care and assistance needs arise.

Plan designs and pricing structures for CCAH programs vary. Depending on the selected plan, a one-time enrollment fee and monthly fee are common, both of which are significantly lower than the entry fee and monthly service fees required for those who ultimately move into the community. Some programs may offer a co-pay pricing model, with the amount of co-pay varying among the types of services.

If the member ultimately wishes to move to the CCRC, they will have priority over non-members, and the monthly service fee will remain the same as it was while the member was living at home, except for inflationary increases.

From an organizational standpoint, CCAH programs can pose financial challenges because accurately projecting long-term care costs for participants is difficult, especially since some may require extensive and expensive services over time. Unlike traditional CCRCs that typically have larger resident populations to spread out financial risk, CCAH programs often serve smaller groups, making them more vulnerable to the impact of high-cost cases.

Additionally, depending on the state, these programs may be subject to strict regulatory requirements, including maintaining financial reserves similar to those required of CCRCs—a requirement that can be challenging to meet, particularly for newer or smaller programs. These factors can make it challenging to maintain the financial sustainability of a CCAH offering over the long term, although some of the more established programs have been in existence for nearly 40 years.

CHAPTER 5

What Else Should I Know About Continuing Care Retirement Communities?

CCRC residents place their trust in the community to provide housing and healthcare for an extended period, usually for the remainder of their lives. While CCRCs want assurance that a new resident's finances are sufficient to cover community costs, prospective residents should also verify the community's financial position to ensure it is well-positioned to uphold its commitments. It's also important to research the quality of healthcare provided. After all, access to healthcare is one of the main reasons for choosing a continuing care retirement community.

Financial viability

When asked about the financial risk of CCRCs, industry representatives often describe how only a small percentage of providers have experienced bankruptcy, historically hovering around 1% of all CCRCs. (Since 2020, there have been approximately 16 CCRCs out of more than 2,000 that have declared bankruptcy.[40])

But it's also important to know that a CCRC can experience financial distress without filing for bankruptcy. In this case, a reorganization of debt or another entity's takeover of a struggling community could occur, while outright bankruptcy is avoided. Yet, the reorganization process could result in fewer services or an increase in monthly service fees (or both), and added stress for residents. In the worst case, the occurrence of either scenario could potentially result in the loss of an entry fee refund.

During and after the Great Recession and housing crisis of 2007-2008, there was an increase in CCRC bankruptcies, often affecting newly developed CCRCs. In many cases, it was a matter of unfortunate timing where communities opened at or near the height of the recession and didn't achieve occupancy fast enough to meet their financial obligations.

Unlike the low inventory housing environment of recent years, in which houses often sell within days or weeks, one of the main drivers of financial difficulties during the Great Recession and corresponding housing crisis was the sudden inability of prospective residents to sell their current homes and use that equity to pay the CCRC entry fee.

As a result, some CCRCs that had waiting lists in the past found themselves struggling to fill new units. Average occupancy ratios across the CCRC industry declined from a peak of around 93% before the recession to a low of approximately 87% in 2010. It is worth noting that this dip in occupancy was in line with what was experienced by independent living communities over the same period.

In the years following the Great Recession, the CCRC industry recovered and eventually surpassed pre-recession levels while keeping bankruptcies largely at bay. And then in 2020, the COVID-19 pandemic unexpectedly hit. According to NIC, occupancy across all CCRCs fell to around 84%—even lower than during the Great Recession. For-profit CCRCs experienced a deeper decline than nonprofits, falling to just under 80% occupancy compared to about 86% for nonprofit CCRCs.

CCRCs with a higher concentration of skilled nursing, where skilled nursing beds represent more than 20% of all living units, experienced the most significant financial strain during the COVID outbreak due largely to increased labor turnover and costs, rising inflation, increased regulatory costs, and limited pricing flexibility due to non-negotiable Medicare and Medicaid reimbursement rates.[43] (Medicare and Medicaid would not be applicable in private-pay CCRCs.)

As a result, some CCRCs have reduced the number of skilled nursing beds available within their community. Others have even chosen to drop skilled nursing entirely, opting instead to offer enhanced or higher acuity assisted living. This is not necessarily the preferred choice of the provider. Afterall, offering a full continuum of care is one of the key attributes and selling points of a CCRC. However, it is a choice often made out of necessity to avoid more profound financial difficulties.

In the years following the COVID-19 outbreak, as the staffing environment has become increasingly challenging, financially strained CCRCs have increasingly sought mergers with larger, more stable providers as a strategy for long-term sustainability. Additionally, there are a growing number of instances where for-profit senior living organizations are acquiring financially impaired nonprofit continuing care retirement communities. In such cases, services may be reduced, or the contract may be reworked. In some situations, even financially stable nonprofit providers are choosing to divest some of their assets or locations as part of a broader strategic realignment.

Navigating a CCRC's financial viability

What are some key factors to consider when determining if a CCRC is financially viable and well-positioned to weather economic downturns? Several factors could ultimately impact the financial stability of a CCRC, many of which are beyond the scope of this book. However, I want to provide a few guidelines to help you get started.

There are both qualitative and quantitative aspects that apply when researching the financial stability of a CCRC. I want to emphasize that it is essential not to place too much weight on any one of the following items, as very few communities will excel in every single area. Instead, you should consider the strength of these components as a whole. Be sure to see the Resources section at the back of the book to find out where you can learn more.

Leadership

The leadership team of a CCRC includes management personnel and, in the case of a nonprofit, the board of directors. Some providers are self-managed, while others hire outside management companies. One isn't necessarily better than the other, but you should ask about the management team's track record in managing CCRCs in good and bad economic times.

The management team and members of the board of directors should have diverse experience in various business sectors, including healthcare and long-term care, insurance, real estate, finance, hospitality management, accounting, and other relevant fields. A board of directors, for example, could have the best volunteers and community leaders, but without an understanding of the organizational and financial structures of CCRCs, they may be limited in their ability to provide proper financial guidance and oversight, especially since the finances of a CCRC are different from a typical operating company.

Or consider a situation where a traditional nursing home provider develops a CCRC. Perhaps the CEO is well-versed in running nursing homes, but that may not translate to operating a CCRC, whereby maintaining strong demand for independent living is critical to success.

The same could be said for a new religious-affiliated CCRC. The executive director or CEO may have been successful in running a church, but that's much different from successfully running a CCRC.

Lastly, consider whether the CCRC board is culturally diverse. A culturally diverse board can help increase employee retention, improve staff members' productivity, and foster an inclusive environment that encourages innovation.

Start-up communities

Bond defaults and other financial challenges often occur when start-up communities fail to reach projected occupancy levels within the expected timeframe. This makes it especially important to evaluate the financials of newer communities carefully—typically those developed within the last six to seven years—as they often carry higher levels of debt. While higher debt isn't inherently problematic, it must be supported by adequate cash flow and steady progress toward occupancy or "fill-up" goals.

Be sure to ask whether the developer has contributed equity or primarily relied on borrowed funds, and how the organization plans to respond if demand falls short of market projections. If management underestimates the time required to fill units and depletes funds before achieving financial sustainability, the risk of default increases.

Rated debt

Although this typically only applies to about 20 to 30% of all CCRCs at any given time, some organizations that finance development or expansion using debt may choose to have their debt rated by one of the major rating agencies, such as Standard & Poor's or Fitch. The debt rating is a strong indicator of a community's financial stability, and therefore its ability to cover the debt payments.

All bond ratings fall under one of two categories: investment-grade and speculative (non-investment-grade). A rating of BBB or higher represents investment-grade debt, indicating a stronger financial outlook and generally the only quality of debt eligible for purchase by large institutions, such as banks or insurance companies.

Fitch Ratings often puts out notices on their rated debt that show whether they have chosen to upgrade, downgrade, or maintain the CCRC's bond rating. CCRCs with the cash flow to meet expenses without taking on too much debt have a good chance of acquiring and maintaining (or even upgrading) an investment-grade rating.

Waitlist

A strong waitlist at a CCRC indicates high demand, especially if securing a spot requires a non-refundable deposit. A waitlist that only requires a small *refundable* deposit may not indicate true demand for the community because it does not require the same level of commitment as a non-refundable deposit.

Unless there has been gross financial mismanagement, a community that maintains high demand over time should generally boast a stronger financial position. Keep in mind, of course, that demand and the strength of a waitlist can change due to market conditions, competition, and other factors.

Accreditation

Is the community accredited by the Continuing Care Accreditation Commission (CCAC)? The CCAC is a division of the Commission on Accreditation of Rehabilitation Facilities (CARF) and is currently the only national accrediting body for continuing care retirement communities.

CARF accreditation remains a topic of debate within the CCRC industry. Because it is voluntary and involves a significant investment of time and resources, many financially sound communities may choose not to pursue it. At the same time, obtaining accreditation should not be viewed as a guarantee of a community's long-term financial stability. While the application process does include a financial review, it also covers many other aspects of the community's operations. Ultimately, the presence or absence of accreditation should be considered as just one of many factors when evaluating the finances of a CCRC.

Type of residency contract(s)

Lifecare (Type A) contracts—and to a lesser degree modified (Type B) contracts—carry more of a financial burden for the provider offering these contracts than do fee-for-service (Type C) contracts because a resident's monthly service fees do not cover the full cost of care at the time those services are received. This means that prudent financial and actuarial practices are especially important for CCRCs offering Type A and Type B contracts, ensuring that funds are available to cover the difference without causing financial strain to the organization.

On the other hand, residents should understand that under a fee-for-service (Type C) contract, the reduction in risk for the retirement community comes about by shifting that risk to the residents. Residents who accept riskier contracts should have the financial wherewithal to sustain that risk, particularly if they require care over a lengthy period.

Refundable entry fee contracts

CCRCs offering large refundable entry fee contracts may face an additional financial burden. Refundable entry fees are recorded as long-term liabilities on a CCRC's balance sheet. Without adequate reserves, these obligations can jeopardize the community's financial stability.

As described in Chapter 4, CCRCs often rely heavily on funds from new residents to fulfill refund commitments, which could become unsustainable if demand for the community declines.

Occupancy level

Maintaining a high level of stabilized occupancy is crucial for CCRCs, as empty units can be a significant financial drain. Rating agencies have traditionally looked for occupancy levels above 90% across all levels of care as part of their rating process.

Consider not only the occupancy level today, but the long-term average and the trend over the past few years. A provider that has experienced low occupancy recently but has taken the appropriate steps to position the community for growth should not necessarily be discounted. Appropriate steps may include hiring new management or an experienced sales director, preparing a new marketing plan by a professional firm with industry experience, implementing plans for renovations, and more.

Marketing/strategic plans

To maintain consistent demand in the marketplace and achieve high occupancy levels, which are critical to long-term success, CCRCs must have up-to-date marketing and strategic plans in place. The CCRC provider should have a deep understanding of its target market's size, needs, and preferences, as well as how the community will continue to position itself as a forward-thinking organization. All of this should be well-articulated in plans for new services, concepts, and physical designs.

Of course, keep in mind too that overly optimistic marketing projections are one of the main reasons why start-up or expansion projects fail.

Financial ratios

You may wish to have a financial professional who is well-versed in CCRCs help you analyze a community's financial ratios, which encompass liquidity, debt, and operating margins (although admittedly, many financial professionals do not have an in-depth understanding of the unique nature of a CCRC's financial model). Examples of key financial ratios include days' cash on hand, cash-to-debt ratio, debt service coverage, and net operating margins, among others. These ratios will help to reveal whether there is an acceptable balance among levels of cash, debt, and operating margins. CARF provides a very helpful guide that goes into more detail on what these ratios mean and how they're calculated. See the Resources section at the back of this book for where to find that.

It is also important to know whether the organization relies heavily on entry fees or investment income to cover operating expenses. If a CCRC becomes overly dependent on these sources of cash to meet operating expenses, it can put the organization at risk over the long term, particularly if challenging economic times lead to a decrease in new entry fees or investment returns.

If a CCRC is part of a multi-site parent organization, it is important to consider the finances of the overall operation, in addition to those of the community itself. Be sure to ask what responsibility the sponsoring organization will accept if a CCRC in its network becomes financially impaired and if this could lead to a reduction of funding at other locations.

Future service obligation

Continuing care retirement communities should assess whether the expected future costs for housing and healthcare are within their anticipated future revenues. If the expected long-term cost of services exceeds expected revenues, it is referred to as a future service obligation (FSO), which should show up on the balance sheet as a long-term liability.

Actuarial analysis

An actuarial analysis performed by a qualified actuary will assess other factors not covered in a basic FSO calculation, including long-term debt, capital expenditures, and planned expansions. The report should indicate that future obligations to current residents are covered, that new resident fees are adequate, and that positive cash flows are projected for the long term.

An actuarial analysis should be performed every few years, and some states now require that the results of these studies be submitted as part of their annual review and oversight process. The CCRC may not make the full actuarial report available to prospective residents but should at least be able to let you know when such a report was last performed and a general summary of the results.

Bond covenants

CCRCs that utilize public debt financing must meet bond covenants established by the bond trustee. Many covenants, which include financial ratios like those mentioned above, are monitored by the issuer. If a CCRC provider has violated a bond covenant, it could be a red flag; however, some violations are minor and are addressed promptly. Any such violations are typically disclosed in the audited financial statements under the footnotes to long-term debt.

There are additional factors that can impact financial stability beyond what is described in this chapter, but if a CCRC receives good marks in most of these areas, it is reasonable to assume that management is taking many of the necessary steps to maintain a strong financial outlook. The biggest red flag may be a lack of transparency about financial viability on the part of the staff. If representatives of the community are not open with you or willing to answer questions on this topic, then it should give you pause.

Government regulation of CCRCs

As mentioned previously, CCRCs are regulated at the state level. As of 2024, 41 states and the District of Columbia regulate CCRCs through various state divisions, including the Department of Insurance, Financial Services, Aging Services, or Social Services. The remaining states currently have no regulatory structure in place.

The regulation of continuing care retirement communities primarily focuses on financial oversight of the entire operation, including independent living, and should not be confused with healthcare licensing, which is regulated separately by the state's appropriate licensing body. Additionally, the healthcare center within a CCRC that receives Medicare and/or Medicaid reimbursements must be certified under federal and state guidelines for those programs. However, these agencies do not regulate the operations and financial management of the entire organization.

For those states that regulate CCRCs, the degree of oversight can vary drastically from one state to another, with some providing only minimal oversight. In many states, the regulatory agency requires that a certain level of disclosure, financial and otherwise, be submitted to the state annually and made available to prospective residents. This is typically done through a document called a "disclosure statement."

Disclosure statements describe important contract details and residents' rights, and include the most recent audited financial statements. These statements often contain financial projections for the next five years.

Some states will require a CCRC to meet certain financial benchmarks each year. If the community fails to meet these benchmarks, the regulatory body will place the community under supervision and request a corrective action plan. If these rehabilitation efforts fail, some states—typically those that regulate CCRCs under the Department of Insurance—will activate a receivership process similar to the one used for insurance companies that fail.

If you are evaluating a community in a state that regulates CCRCs, consider reaching out to the relevant regulatory agency to inquire about the financial requirements, oversight process, and any history of bankruptcy among CCRCs in the state. Much of this information may also be available on the state's main website under the section for the division that oversees CCRCs.

Remember, however, that just because a CCRC is in a state that is not regulated, it does not mean that it is poorly managed or financially unstable. There appears to be no recent data indicating that providers located in regulated states perform better financially than those in unregulated states. However, in recent years, many states have increased the reporting requirements and oversight of CCRCs.

Quality of care

While CCRCs often promote appealing services, activities, and amenities for independent living, it's essential to remember that a core reason for choosing this type of community is access to a full continuum of care, including assisted living, memory care, and/or skilled nursing.

Just as you carefully assess the financial aspects of a CCRC, it's equally important to evaluate the quality of the healthcare services. Are community representatives eager and transparent when discussing their healthcare offerings? Do they proudly showcase their healthcare center or seem reluctant to mention it? What sets their care services, technology, and facility design apart from others? Keep in mind that even an older building can still house exceptional care, while a new facility doesn't automatically guarantee high-quality service. Ultimately, the most important determinant of quality of care is the availability and reliability of a caring staff.

When evaluating healthcare services in a CCRC, here are a few more things to consider:

CMS rating

If the community is Medicare-certified (as opposed to private-pay), you can check out the healthcare rating from the Centers for Medicare and Medicaid Services (CMS) at Medicare.gov under the section called "Care Compare." In addition to notes on quality measures, safety inspection reports, and more, the CMS rating includes staffing ratios, which reveal the average amount of time per day that residents spend with an RN as opposed to a nurse's aide.

For private pay communities that are not Medicare-certified, CMS does not provide this type of information; however, you can ask the community about how they measure up to those same markers.

Long-term care ombudsman

You may be able to find a list of complaints and other consumer advocacy reports at the long-term care ombudsman program for the state in which the CCRC is located.

Ombudsman representatives serve as volunteer advocates for people living in care facilities. The program offers residents and their loved ones a way to file a formal complaint against an area facility—such as nursing homes, free-standing assisted living facilities, adult care homes, and continuing care retirement communities—and works to resolve the grievance or regulatory violation.

Online reviews

Star ratings and reviews on various third-party websites can be helpful, but keep in mind that people are often more inclined to write a negative review than a good one. Therefore, ratings and reviews are more helpful when there is a large sample size. A small handful of reviews may not accurately reflect the provider's true performance. Even the very best organizations occasionally receive complaints.

Observe for yourself

While some people prefer not to see the healthcare facility until they need care, it can be worthwhile to visit and observe. Observe whether the nursing staff appears happy and productive. Does the facility appear well-kept and free of lingering odors? Do the residents appear well cared for by the staff? Are there any innovative solutions or practices being used to enhance the patient care experience?

Ask others

If you know someone who has received care themselves or has a loved one who has received care in the facility, ask about their experiences. This is one of the very best ways to gain valuable insights into the quality of the healthcare center at a CCRC.

Nonprofit and for-profit CCRCs

Many people wonder about the differences between nonprofit and for-profit CCRC organizations, and how the differences should factor into a potential resident's decision-making process.

As mentioned in Chapter 3, approximately 80% of CCRCs today maintain a nonprofit tax status. Nonprofit CCRCs are typically organized as tax-exempt 501(c)(3) entities and often operate with a strong mission-driven focus, particularly those affiliated with faith-based organizations. Others may not be affiliated with a religious organization but still maintain nonprofit status under a decades-old IRS ruling that considers meeting the needs of the aged a charitable service for federal tax purposes.

One of the more common appeals of a nonprofit CCRC is that all revenue is reinvested back into the organization as opposed to being paid out to owners or investors. An exception to this would be any portion of revenue that goes towards debt service payments.

Executives and a volunteer board of directors typically provide the governance of a nonprofit CCRC. Ideally, there should be at least a couple of residents serving on the board—not as figureheads, but as fully engaged members whose perspectives and input are valued in shaping organizational decisions. Resident board members should be empowered to contribute meaningfully, ensuring their voices influence the strategic direction and oversight of the CCRC. Day-to-day management of a nonprofit CCRC may be handled internally or outsourced to a third-party management company.

For-profit CCRCs, by contrast, are typically owned and operated by corporations or investors. In some cases, the owner may have a long track record of developing and managing senior living communities. In other cases, it could be a real estate investment trust (REIT) or another type of investment fund that owns a significant percentage of the organization and outsources management and operations.

Most for-profit CCRCs are part of larger multi-site organizations. Like any for-profit business, their primary objective is to generate revenue and provide returns to shareholders. This isn't inherently negative, however. A well-managed for-profit organization can achieve strong financial performance while still providing exceptional service to its residents. In fact, over the long term, it would be quite challenging to maintain profitability while also having low resident satisfaction.

Another common difference between nonprofit and for-profit CCRCs is the level of financial support available to residents. Many nonprofit CCRCs maintain a long-standing tradition of not forcing residents to leave due to a lack of funds- an approach that reflects their charitable mission to support older adults in times of need. As a result, nonprofit CCRCs typically offer financial assistance to help residents remain in the community if they exhaust their financial resources through no fault of their own. However, nonprofit communities are still businesses that must be financially responsible. Therefore, nonprofit continuing care contracts often include language such as:

> *"The community may offer financial assistance to a resident who has encountered financial difficulty, provided the resident has managed his or her resources properly after taking occupancy ... such assistance will be conditional on the community's ability to provide funds while operating on a sound financial basis."*

In addition to any internally designated financial assistance funds, many nonprofit CCRCs also maintain benevolent funds or resident-supported endowments to help those in financial distress. Still, the presence of such a fund does not guarantee support. It must be consistently and adequately funded over time. Indeed, a community's ability to provide financial assistance hinges on its overall financial strength and stability.

For-profit CCRCs, in general, are less likely to offer ongoing financial support to residents who have exhausted their assets, making this an important consideration for those concerned about outliving their resources. However, while this level of financial assistance is most common among nonprofit communities, some for-profit CCRCs do provide financial aid or maintain dedicated endowment funds to help residents in financial need.

As with any critical aspect of the CCRC decision-making process, it's important to have a transparent discussion with the community's finance director and, if possible, a resident council or board representative involved in financial matters. Ask about the history of financial aid availability, inquire about the current funding status of any benevolent or endowment funds, and review the specific contract language that governs such assistance.

CHAPTER 6

How Does Long-Term Care Impact My Retirement Housing Choice?

Choosing the retirement living option that best suits your situation depends largely on how you plan to address your future long-term care needs. One of the most important questions is whether you want to live somewhere equipped to provide the care you may need in the future, or whether you prefer to stay in your home with the support of caregivers. While pondering these questions, people often want to know the odds of requiring long-term care, how long it might last, and the cost and resources available to help pay for it.

Before moving on, I want to be clear about what I mean by the phrase "long-term care." Generally, long-term care is defined as care for individuals with chronic conditions, limited physical capabilities, or extended healthcare needs that prevent them from functioning independently on a day-to-day basis. It may include assisted living, memory care, or even skilled nursing care that is necessary for an extended or indefinite period.

As described on the website of the American Association for Long-Term Care Insurance (AALTCI), your risk of needing long-term care is either 0%

(you will never need it) or 100% (you will need it). This is an oversimplification, but the point is that your plans should not rely too heavily on averages, as your individual experience may not align with them. Also, when considering data on long-term care, remember that current data is mainly based on previous generations, who, on average, did not live as long or experience as many chronic health conditions as current and future generations likely will.

Surprisingly, there isn't a lot of up-to-date and detailed information publicly available relating to the odds of needing long-term care in various settings nor average lengths of stay. The most popular study, and the one most often referenced by the Centers for Medicare and Medicaid Services (CMS), was published in the healthcare journal INQUIRY in 2005, revealing that nearly 70% of people over age 65 will require long-term care services during their lifetime, with 79% of women and 58% of men requiring long-term care.[44] It should be noted that the definition of "assistance" used in this study is quite broad, including those requiring hands-on assistance not only with activities of daily (ADLs), but also instrumental activities of daily living (IADLs). Most studies before this one focused primarily on nursing home usage since in-home care and assisted living communities were not as prevalent.

Recognizing the lack of comprehensive and up-to-date data on the lifetime risk that older adults will need long-term supports and services (LTSS), the Office of Disability, Aging, and Long-Term Care Policy under the Department of Health and Human Services (HHS) released a report in 2019 based on a longitudinal household survey.[45] Different from the INQUIRY report, this research defines long-term supports and services (LTSS) as: (1) having difficulty with two or more ADLs that are expected to last at least 90 days or severe cognitive impairment; and (2) receiving unpaid care from family or friends, or paid care in a facility or at home.

The HHS report found that approximately 70% of adults who survive to age 65 develop severe LTSS needs before they die, and that 48% of those requiring LTSS receive some form of paid care over their lifetime. However, the findings also revealed that the lifetime risk of receiving paid care is not evenly distributed across the population. Longer spates of severe LTSS were found to be much more common among older adults with fewer financial resources than their wealthier counterparts.

A more recent study was released in 2025 by the Center for Retirement Research at Boston College, which found that around 80% of all people 65 and older will need long-term care at some point over their remaining lifetime.[46]

Another way to potentially assess the odds of needing long-term care is to evaluate the experience of long-term care insurance (LTCI) policyholders. According to the AALTCI, 35 to 50% of people who own long-term care insurance will use the policy, depending on the elimination period.[47] The elimination period is essentially a deductible but is based on the number of days you are required to pay for care out of pocket before your benefits begin. A common elimination period is 90 days. Because some policyholders may only require care for a short time—less than the elimination period—their benefits are never triggered, and they are not counted in the 35 to 50% who ultimately use their coverage. If the data by AALTCI also included those receiving care during the elimination period, then the percentage of those requiring care would be considerably higher.

Keep in mind that long-term care insurance can only be purchased when someone is generally healthy. If we were to factor in those who could not qualify for coverage (or afford it) but still eventually needed long-term care then the overall percentage of people requiring assistance would be higher, likely bringing the total back up to around the same 70 to 80% range.

Yet, these statistics do not answer another important question: How long do people need long-term care?

According to the latest research by the U.S. Administration on Aging (AOA), individuals who require long-term care in any setting typically need it for approximately three years. Specifically, women require an average of 3.7 years of care, while men require 2.2 years of care.[48]

Like the 2005 INQUIRY journal study, this AOA research includes not only those requiring help with ADLs but also those requiring help with IADLs. Approximately 45% of individuals receiving paid care will initially receive it in their own homes, typically for less than a year. Those receiving unpaid care from friends or family will typically receive care at home for a period of one to two years. Presumably, this data comes from government Medicare and Medicaid records, although the AOA website does not cite the source of the data.

Looking specifically at the average time spent in an assisted living community, data provided by the American Health Care Association (AHCA) and the National Center for Assisted Living (NCAL) shows the median stay to be around 22 months[49], but this doesn't account for the fact that the average length of stay can also vary by gender, income, pre-existing conditions, and age. Typically, the older the resident, the less time they will spend in assisted living. The data also show that about one-third of people aged 65 and over will never need long-term care, and around 20% will require care for more than five years.

However, long-term care does not always end with assisted living. According to the same AHCA/NCAL study, nearly 60% of all assisted living residents eventually transition to a skilled nursing facility, also known as a nursing home. Separately, the AOA report indicates that the average stay in a skilled nursing facility is approximately one year; however, the nursing facility figures are not broken down by short-term (rehab) stays and permanent stays, nor by gender, ethnicity, or income. If we were to remove short-term rehab stays, the average skilled nursing stay would be considerably longer.

Lastly, the previously referenced study, prepared by the Center for Retirement Research at Boston College, found that approximately 40% of individuals requiring long-term care will require high-intensity care for more than a year.

In summary, it is not unreasonable to expect that a person may receive care at home for several months or longer, followed by another year or two in an assisted living community, with almost 60% then requiring a nursing home stay that could range anywhere from a few weeks up to several years, depending on the situation.

I want to reiterate that, although understanding these statistics is helpful, your personal experience or that of a loved one may fall significantly outside the averages in either direction.

What does long-term care cost?

As described in Chapter 1, the 2024 national average cost for a home health aide was $6,292 per month (based on 44 hours per week), and the base monthly rate for a room in an assisted living community was $5,900.[13] These figures can be significantly higher depending on the level of services required, the quality of the provider, and the region. A comprehensive health assessment is a crucial step in determining the level of care a resident requires and the associated costs.

It is also important to understand that most assisted living providers charge a base monthly rate for core services but then charge separately for additional ancillary services such as medication management, specialized meal plans, laundry services, and transportation. In this case, the main thing to understand is what services are included in the published rate and what services will be an extra cost. Other assisted living providers operate under an all-inclusive model whereby nearly all services are included in the monthly cost. Understanding these different approaches to pricing is helpful when comparing costs.

Regarding skilled nursing care, the national average for a semi-private room in a nursing home was $9,277 per month in 2024, and for a private room it was $10,646 per month, although it is not uncommon for the monthly cost of skilled nursing care to exceed $15,000 in some areas of the country.

The Genworth/CareScout study, referenced in the Resources section of this book, provides state-by-state averages for various types of care.

Paying for senior living and long-term care services

Many people are confused or misinformed about the various options that are available (or not available) to help pay for long-term care services. The sources of payment for long-term care services can be categorized into two main groups: public (government-funded) programs and private pay. In this chapter, we'll cover the public programs, including Medicare, Medicaid, and the Department of Veterans Affairs (VA). Private pay options, covered in the following chapter, include paying out of pocket, using a long-term care insurance policy, and possibly accessing the cash value in a life insurance policy.

Public Programs

Medicare

Medicare is a federal health insurance program that mostly provides healthcare coverage for those age 65 and older. According to a 2023 report prepared by the Associated Press and the NORC Center for Public Affairs Research, 45% of people age 65-plus believe Medicare will pay for any long-term care services received in a nursing home.[50] A separate survey of baby boomers by Bankers Life revealed that more than 55% mistakenly believe Medicare will cover long-term care services in *any* setting.[51] These last two statistics indicate a major misconception among the public: that Medicare will cover long-term care or skilled nursing care indefinitely.

Medicare Part A and Part B are often referred to as "traditional Medicare." Part A is hospital coverage, and Part B is outpatient physician coverage. Medicare supplement plans or "Med-Sup Plans," which are available through private insurance companies, cover gaps that Parts A and B may not include, such as co-insurance, co-pays, and deductibles. Regarding long-term care, the key point to understand about Medicare is that it covers only *medically necessary* care. It does *not* cover assisted living (non-medical supportive services) if that's the only type of care needed.

Medicare Part A will cover medically necessary skilled nursing care, but only for a limited time and in a limited amount, and only when certain stipulations have been met. Medicare's goal is to help patients recover as quickly as possible, which is why the term "rehab" is commonly used when referring to Medicare coverage of skilled nursing care.

Here are a few of the qualifications that must be met before Medicare will cover skilled nursing care services:

- Care must be provided in a Medicare-certified facility. (Medically necessary services provided at home by a Medicare-certified home healthcare agency may also qualify for Medicare coverage.)
- The recipient of care must have first had an "admitted" hospital stay of at least three days or longer, none of which can be considered "observation" days.
- Admittance into the skilled nursing facility must take place within 30 days of the hospital stay.

- A physician must decide that daily medical nursing care or rehab is necessary.

Referencing Genworth/CareScout's Cost of Care Survey again, the average national daily rate for skilled (medically necessary) nursing care in 2024—including the cost of a semi-private room, meals, therapies, medications, and more—was $305. For those who meet the qualifications listed above, Medicare may cover the full cost of medical care for the first 20 days.

Between days 21 and 100, Medicare paid $204 per day in 2024 with the patient paying the difference, although it is *not guaranteed* that Medicare will provide coverage over this entire 100 days. The actual number of days covered by Medicare depends on whether the patient requires continued skilled nursing or therapy services. If it is determined by Medicare that such care is no longer medically reasonable or necessary, or if the patient has reached a "plateau" or is deemed "maintenance only," meaning they no longer need skilled care to improve or safely maintain their condition, then Medicare may cease to cover the cost of care.

Additionally, if skilled nursing care is required for *more than* 100 days, then Medicare ceases to provide coverage regardless of the need. At that point, the recipient of services is required to pay 100% of the cost out of pocket. However, the 100-day period can reset in certain situations if at least 60 days pass between occurrences.

Also, keep in mind that the rate shown above only covers the cost of a *semi-private* room. Residents who choose a private room will have to pay the difference out of pocket. In 2024, the average national rate for a private nursing care room was $350 per day, compared to $305 for a semi-private room.

Medicaid

Unlike Medicare, which is a federal program, Medicaid is administered at the state level, although it does receive federal funding. The key difference is that Medicaid is designed specifically for low-income households to help pay for medical expenses.

In contrast to Medicare, Medicaid will pay for skilled nursing AND assisted living care, potentially for an unlimited duration. This care is usually provided in a facility setting, although financial assistance is increasingly being made available for in-home care through sources such as the Program for All-Inclusive Care for the Elderly (PACE). (See the Resources section in the back of this book to learn more about PACE.)

Medicaid eligibility requirements vary by state, but suffice it to say that, except for a few allowances, qualifying for Medicaid requires that you have exhausted most of your financial resources, and your income must be close to the federal poverty level. (Most states allow the cost of care to be deducted against income when determining if income eligibility requirements are met.) Additionally, Medicaid will only cover long-term care services if your provider—either the facility or a home care provider—is certified by Medicaid.

Since the passing of the Affordable Care Act (ACA) in 2010, states that chose to expand Medicaid have generally had less restrictive eligibility requirements compared to non-expansion states. As of 2024, 41 states, including the District of Columbia, have adopted Medicaid expansion under the ACA—a significant increase from just 12 states in 2016 when the last edition of this book was being written.[51]

However, this trend toward broader Medicaid access may now be reversing. A recently enacted federal spending package includes significant cuts to Medicaid, raising concerns about the future of coverage for low-income individuals, including older adults who rely on Medicaid for long-term care services. While the full impact of these cuts remains to be seen, they could prompt states to reassess eligibility criteria or reduce program benefits, potentially limiting access for individuals who would have previously qualified. It is projected that already struggling hospitals and nursing homes in rural parts of the country will be hardest hit by these funding reductions.

Since Medicaid is designed to help those most financially in need, the government discourages people from giving away assets to qualify. A detailed discussion is beyond the scope of this book, but you should know that if you apply for Medicaid, there will be a five-year look-back period that begins immediately preceding the time of the application. Representatives of Medicaid will analyze your personal finances to determine if any assets were given away during that time. If so, you will face a transfer penalty, which means you will first be required to pay for your care up to an amount that is approximately equal to the amount you gave away before Medicaid begins to pay. Furthermore, this approach to paying for care also limits the options available as it would only include Medicaid-certified providers.

Department of Veterans Affairs (the VA)

Qualifying Veterans and their surviving spouses are sometimes unaware of a valuable benefit available through the Office of Veterans Affairs' Administration's Aid and Attendance Program, which helps cover the cost of assisted living in a facility or at home.

Qualification is not dependent on service-related injuries and can provide upwards of $34,000 in annual benefits, with caps ranging from $1,500 to $2,800 per month, depending on income levels and whether the recipient is married, single, or a surviving spouse of a Veteran. This is usually not enough to cover the full cost of nursing home care, but it can help preserve one's assets for a longer period and can have a bigger impact when applied to less expensive care, such as assisted living or in-home care. A detailed analysis of qualifications can be found by referencing the Resources section at the back of this book, but in addition to service requirements and income and asset limits, eligibility generally requires that the recipient either needs assistance from another person for everyday activities of daily living (ADLs), is bedridden, is living in a nursing home, OR is legally blind.

Some Veterans who already qualify for Medicaid may feel applying for VA benefits is a useless exercise. Still, there may be other benefits to doing so, and it is important to explore all possible avenues when it comes to paying for long-term care.

CHAPTER 7

What are Other Ways of Paying for Long-Term Care or Funding a Move to a Retirement Community?

In the previous chapter, I described the public-pay options for covering the cost of long-term care. In this chapter, I'll review the private-pay options. The term "private pay" generally means paying for necessary assisted living services or skilled nursing care using your own financial resources, without the assistance of government programs. Importantly, if a care facility describes itself as private pay, it means that the facility does not accept Medicare and/or Medicaid reimbursements.

Keep in mind that some of the options described in this chapter may also be used to cover the cost of moving to a continuing care retirement community or another senior living option, even when long-term care is not needed. While many prospective residents of a retirement community will sell their home and use the proceeds to fund a move, this may not always be an option. Therefore, it's helpful to understand the other alternatives.

Let's look at some of the main private pay options.

Long-term care insurance (LTCI)

Long-term care insurance (LTCI) is most suitable for individuals who maintain a financial standing well above the level at which they would qualify for Medicaid, but not high enough to cover the out-of-pocket costs of care over an extended period. It's also suitable for those who have sufficient savings and assets to cover the cost of care out of pocket but prefer to leave money to loved ones or charity instead of incurring the full expense of care. Carving out a small fraction of one's assets to pay for long-term care insurance could prevent spending a much larger share of their assets on care later.

The ideal time to purchase long-term care insurance is typically between the ages of mid-50s to early 60s. If you're beyond that age, you can still obtain coverage if you qualify, but justifying the higher premiums may become more difficult.

In the early days of long-term care insurance, most policies were considered pure nursing home policies, meaning they only covered the cost of care in a nursing home. But most LTCI policies issued over the past 20 years or so also cover assisted living and in-home care.

LTCI policies have certain "triggers" that must be met for a policyholder to be eligible for a claim. For most policies, a common trigger is the inability to perform at least two, or sometimes three, of the activities of daily living (ADLs) without assistance.

As with any type of insurance, the decision to own LTCI is essentially a decision to cap the level of risk one is willing to take with their money and transfer the remaining risk to a third party. However, LTCI policies are not one-size-fits-all; there are numerous features to consider when purchasing a policy, including the amount of daily or monthly coverage, elimination period (the duration during which you will pay for your care before coverage begins), number of years of coverage, inflation protection, and more.

Many of the newer LTCI policies are non-traditional and generally offer a combination of life insurance or an annuity alongside LTCI. With these hybrid plans, you may not get as much long-term care coverage per dollar as you would with a traditional plan, but they offer other benefits not available with traditional LTCI plans, such as cash value buildup and death benefits.

In recent years, the LTCI industry has faced significant headwinds. The combination of overly optimistic business judgments, actuarial miscalculations, higher-than-expected policy retention rates, and a prolonged low-interest rate environment has led many carriers to increase premiums dramatically and others to drop out of the business altogether. This has impacted individual policyholders, as well as group LTCI programs such as the federal employees' LTCI program.

Despite the recent challenges, LTCI is likely to remain a viable option among those whose assets are too high to qualify for Medicaid but too low to self-insure against the costs of years of long term care. When LTCI coverage is maintained and ultimately used, the benefits usually far outweigh the costs, even with the steep premium increases consumers have faced in recent years. Of course, if paying the premium becomes a financial hardship for the policyholder, then it may not be feasible to maintain the coverage.

Many states have introduced Long-Term Care Partnership Programs, also known as Qualified State Long-Term Care Partnership Programs, to encourage the purchase of long-term care insurance. However, there still appears to be little awareness of these programs. A partnership-qualified long-term care insurance policy can protect your assets up to an amount that is roughly equivalent to the coverage provided by the policy *if* you exhaust your assets on care *and* subsequently qualify for Medicaid. (See the

Resources section of this book for more information on LTCI Partnership Programs.)

When choosing a long-term care insurance policy, be sure to work with an experienced and reputable agent or financial planner to help evaluate your choices and find a plan that is suitable for your unique situation. If you already own an LTCI policy, be sure you know exactly what it covers and does not cover, as well as the other details mentioned above. It's best not to wait until you need to use your policy to learn what it covers.

The relationship between long-term care insurance and CCRC lifecare (Type A) contracts

Before moving on to other types of private pay options, it is helpful to understand a little more about how LTCI works with CCRCs that offer a lifecare contract. As outlined in Chapter 4, CCRC residents who select a traditional lifecare (Type A) contract generally do not experience an increase in their monthly fees when long-term care services are needed, aside from inflationary adjustments and potential ancillary costs. As a result, some may question whether purchasing or maintaining long-term care insurance is necessary if they also have a lifecare contract through a CCRC.

Indeed, a lifecare contract functions much like an unlimited long-term care insurance policy. However, if you already own LTCI coverage, there are several reasons why it may still be worthwhile to keep it even if you obtain a lifecare contract at a CCRC.

After being approved for a long-term care insurance claim and meeting the elimination period, CCRC residents who hold a lifecare contract are often able to use their LTCI coverage to offset the monthly service fee at the lifecare community. In this scenario, even though the resident's monthly service fee does not increase when care services are received, much of the monthly fee may still be offset by their long-term care insurance benefit.

This could result in a situation where the net monthly cost while receiving care, after factoring in the long-term care insurance benefit, would be substantially lower than before receiving care.

Maintaining LTCI coverage with a lifecare contract could be particularly beneficial if you own a "cash-benefit" policy. Although not as common with newer policies, cash-benefit policies pay a fixed amount directly to the policyholder after a claim is approved, as opposed to a "reimbursement policy," in which claims are limited to the higher of the long-term care expenses or the maximum policy benefit. It is conceivable that in some cases the cash-benefit coverage amount could be higher than the monthly service fee being paid at the CCRC.

In the case of a reimbursement policy, you should find out from the CCRC how they calculate the portion of your monthly service fee that may be submitted to a long-term care insurance carrier for reimbursement.

There are also other reasons to consider keeping your LTCI coverage. Suppose, for instance, that the lifecare contract's healthcare benefit only applies to care received in the on-site healthcare facility, but a resident decides that he or she would like to hire a home healthcare worker to provide services in their independent living unit for a few hours each day. In this case, they would be required to pay out of pocket for these charges and thus could potentially use LTCI to cover some or all of the cost.

Or suppose a CCRC resident with a lifecare contract decides to move out of the community because they are either unhappy or facing extenuating circumstances. If the resident moves to another retirement community, they may be required to pay the full market rate for healthcare services eventually needed, but would no longer have their long-term care insurance policy to help cover the cost.

Regardless of whether the CCRC you are considering offers a lifecare or fee-for-service contract, or both, be sure to speak with a representative of the retirement community—preferably someone on the executive or finance team—and inquire about how the community provides support for filing LTCI claims. It is worth noting that some CCRCs will accept the assignment of your LTCI benefits and reduce your fee obligations proportionately. Also, find out if the CCRC has had any specific instances with other residents whereby they have not been able to utilize their LTCI coverage or were limited in using the full benefit.

It is also highly advisable to have a conversation with your LTCI agent or a member of the claims team to find out if there are any restrictions on coverage as it relates to services provided in a continuing care retirement community. Find out exactly what they need from you and/or the facility to process a claim and if your policy classifies CCRCs under home care, assisted living community care, skilled nursing facility care, or all the above (as your needs change). Some older LTCI policies may classify CCRC services as an "alternate care benefit" or "alternative" care. Policy definitions and classifications could impact your ability to receive benefits. If your policy does not mention CCRCs and how they are classified, you may want to ask a representative of the insurance company to provide a written explanation for your records.

Reverse mortgages

The reverse mortgage has emerged as an increasingly popular option for paying for long-term care services, thanks to the introduction of new features, stricter regulations, and lower fees.

Usually designed for homeowners age 62 and older, reverse mortgages provide either a lump sum or a string of payments over time. The allowable amount is based on a certain percentage of equity in your home, which could be up to 60% or more, depending on your age, whether you have an outstanding mortgage or liens on the property, and current interest rates.

The main difference between a reverse mortgage and a traditional home equity line of credit (HELOC) is that with a reverse mortgage, the line of credit is not due until you move out of your home or at death, in which case your heirs or your estate could pay the loan back by selling the home, or by any other means.

While a reverse mortgage includes many of the same costs and fees as a traditional mortgage, such as origination fees and closing costs, it also has additional expenses that can increase the overall cost. (See the Resources section at the back of this book for more information on reverse mortgages.)

Withdrawals from investments

Paying out of pocket for long-term care, or to fund a move to a continuing care retirement community, often means withdrawing funds from savings, investments, or retirement accounts. One of the biggest considerations of this option is the potential tax impact of these withdrawals.

Withdrawals from a taxable account will typically be taxed much differently than withdrawals from tax-deferred vehicles, such as an individual retirement account (IRA). Withdrawals from taxable accounts often involve either the sale or redemption of shares from traditional securities like stocks, exchange-traded funds (ETFs), or mutual funds. They may also include the withdrawal of previously taxed dividends, capital gains, and interest payments reinvested into the account or fund.

Withdrawals and investment redemptions from a taxable account will generally be taxed as capital gains, assuming there is a gain. Simply put: A capital gain is the difference between what is paid for an investment and the price at which it is sold.

As of 2025, the *long-term* capital gains tax, which applies to the sale of an investment held for longer than a year, ranges from 0% to 20%, depending on the account holder's total annual income and income bracket. If you're in a higher ordinary income tax bracket, you will pay a higher capital gains tax, but if your annual income is lower, then you'll pay a lower capital gains tax, and possibly no capital gains tax at all.

As with most financial and tax-related topics, there are exceptions. For example, investments classified as "collectibles" may have a capital gains tax rate higher than 20%. The *short-term* capital gains tax, which applies to the sale of an investment held for one year or less, is generally taxed as ordinary income and not as capital gain. Before selling stocks or mutual funds in a taxable account, it's important to know whether it will generate a capital gains tax.

Keep in mind that an investor can also have a capital *loss* when an investment is sold for less than its cost. Long-term capital losses can often be used to offset long-term capital gains. Working with an experienced financial professional to identify which shares have the largest gains and whether there are applicable carry-over losses can help minimize the payment of unnecessary taxes. Furthermore, a knowledgeable advisor should understand the nuances and various exceptions that may apply to your situation.

As mentioned previously, withdrawals from a taxable account may include the withdrawal of dividends, capital gains, and interest that have been reinvested into the account, which would have been taxed at that time. In this case, there would likely be no taxes due on that part of the withdrawal. With a few exceptions, most dividends paid by stocks and mutual funds are taxed at the prevailing long-term capital gains rate in the year received. The interest paid on bonds or bond funds, however, is usually taxed as ordinary income, except in the case of tax-free municipal bonds. As with stocks, selling a bond or bond fund will also be subject to capital gains or losses in the year it is sold.

One last word on redemptions and withdrawals from taxable accounts: If your modified adjusted gross income (MAGI) exceeds certain thresholds, you may owe an additional 3.8% (in 2025) net investment income tax (NIIT).

Withdrawals from tax-deferred accounts

Tax-deferred accounts include individual retirement accounts (IRAs), employer-sponsored retirement plans (such as 401[k]s), and tax-deferred annuities. Except for after-tax contributions to a retirement account, which are rare, withdrawals from tax-deferred accounts will be taxed as ordinary income (as opposed to capital gains). The amount of ordinary income tax due on the withdrawal is based on your MAGI and corresponding tax bracket in the year of withdrawal. Like redemptions from taxable accounts, withdrawals from tax-deferred retirement accounts may also be subject to the NIIT.

Withdrawals from tax-deferred annuities are also subject to ordinary income tax, but it works a little differently from a traditional IRA or 401k, for example. The difference is that taxes are only paid on the growth in the account and not on the amount invested or deposited into the annuity (the cost basis). All contributions to a tax-deferred annuity are considered a return of the principal and therefore are not taxed. The annuity holder generally is required to withdraw all gains before withdrawing contributions. This would not be true, however, if the annuity were held within an IRA.

Life insurance cash values

One of the senior living funding options occasionally considered is a cash-value life insurance policy. Some older adults may have purchased policies years ago that have accumulated significant cash value. If there is no longer a big need for life insurance coverage, then the question may be whether it is reasonable to use the policy's accumulated cash to cover a senior living move.

Here are a few basic details to understand before tapping into a life insurance policy's cash value to pay for your senior living move:

Is there a surrender charge?

Most permanent life insurance policies have a surrender penalty that applies if the policy is cashed out in the early years. In some cases, the surrender period may last as long as 20 years or more. Before cashing out a policy, it's important to be sure there is no applicable surrender penalty to do so.

Does the cash value exceed the amount of total premiums paid?

Hopefully, the answer is yes, but this does mean there can be tax implications of a withdrawal. One nice thing about withdrawals from life insurance cash values is that, under the current tax code, it's treated as first in, first out (FIFO). This means withdrawals are first considered a return of cost basis.

After the cost basis is fully withdrawn, all additional distributions will be taxed as ordinary income. The tax due on these withdrawals will depend on your tax bracket. Also, unlike most retirement accounts and annuities, life insurance withdrawals are not subject to age 59 ½ early withdrawal penalties. *(See the next point for an exception to this.)*

Is the policy a modified endowment policy (MEC)?

Some life insurance policies have flexible premium options. In this case, the policy will have a limit on how much premium you can pay without adverse consequences. If someone "overfunds" a policy, perhaps seeking to capitalize on the tax-advantaged growth, it can be classified as a modified endowment policy (MEC). In this case, withdrawals are taken under last-in, first-out (LIFO), and therefore gains are required to be taken first. Additionally, 59 ½ early withdrawal penalties may apply.

Is it a full or partial withdrawal?

A full withdrawal of the cash value will cause the policy to terminate, which may be okay if it's determined that the coverage isn't needed any longer. A partial withdrawal, however, typically lowers the coverage amount on a dollar-for-dollar basis, although some policies will allow withdrawals up to a certain percentage before this happens.

An alternative to a cash withdrawal would be a loan against the policy. A loan technically does not lower the coverage amount because it can be paid back. However, if the insured should pass away with an outstanding loan, then the loan balance will be deducted from the coverage. Loans are also not taxable when withdrawn. However, if the loan balance accumulates and eventually causes the policy to lapse, it could trigger a taxable event at that time.

Life Settlements

There are companies called life settlement providers or life settlement brokers that will buy a life insurance policy from the policy holder. This, too, could be an option for those who no longer have a need for their life insurance. In the case of a cash-value policy, the life settlement company will typically pay the policyholder *more* than the cash value but *less* than the death benefit, and then the life settlement company is designated as the beneficiary of the policy. Some will also buy certain types of term insurance policies for less than the death benefit. By purchasing the policy, the company will take over the premium payments if premiums are still due on the policy. Essentially, these life settlement businesses operate by making money when the policyholder dies. Though it might sound a little unorthodox, there are legitimate companies that offer this service, but as with most things money-related, there are also scammers, so use caution.

Loan against securities

Some financial institutions—typically larger brokerage houses—offer loans using the investor's securities (stocks, mutual funds, etc.) as collateral. The loans may allow loans up to 60-80% of the account value. This can be a quick way to access funds but it comes with risks related to market volatility. If the value of the account were to decline significantly while the loan is outstanding, the account holder may be required to deposit more funds to maintain the required loan to value ratio. This is commonly referred to as a "margin call."

Bridge loans

A bridge loan can assist with senior living expenses for those planning to sell their home but needing flexibility in timing. Offered by companies specializing in senior living bridge loans or sometimes by local banks, these loans are often used when someone wants to relocate soon but is waiting for assets to become available, such as proceeds from a home sale or other payments. Bridge loans are typically approved quickly, with funds available within days.

These short-term loans, usually secured by home equity or other assets, last between six to eighteen months and tend to have higher interest rates than traditional loans. Payments are often interest-only, with full repayment made in a lump sum once permanent financing is obtained, such as after selling a home. Bridge loans provide flexibility by allowing families or seniors to cover entrance fees, monthly senior living costs, or moving expenses without rushing a home sale or liquidating other assets. However, they are best considered a temporary solution due to their higher costs and the risk of increased debt if expected funds are delayed.

Note: Any of the financial products and options described in this chapter should be discussed with a qualified financial professional and tax advisor before making any decisions. Nothing in this chapter should be considered personal financial advice.

CHAPTER 8

What Will Retirement Communities Look Like in the Future?

There is an ongoing debate about the future growth trajectory of the senior living industry. Many believe that the sheer size of the aging baby boomer population will inevitably lead to a surge in demand for senior housing. This view is supported by demographic projections and industry forecasts such as those highlighted by NIC MAP, a senior housing data and analytics resource, which projects increased occupancy and expansion in the sector due in large part to the shortage of supply.[52]

However, others caution against the assumption that population growth alone will translate into proportional demand for traditional senior living models. Advances in technology, the rise of accessory dwelling units (ADUs), and alternative aging-in-place strategies—such as the village movement and other peer-to-peer support models—are enabling more older adults to remain in their homes for more extended periods. As a result, the senior living industry must look beyond demographic trends and proactively respond to shifting consumer values, preferences, and lifestyles.

While the exact magnitude of future demand may be uncertain, there is little doubt that there will be significant growth opportunities for the most forward-thinking senior living organizations. For providers aiming to meet the evolving demand and thrive in a competitive landscape, success will depend on their ability to innovate while staying attuned to what today's and tomorrow's older adults truly want. This requires more than assumptions about care needs or housing preferences. It calls for meaningful insight into their priorities, motivations, and definitions of well-being.

As the senior living industry prepares for a more engaged and discerning generation of older adults, gaining a deeper understanding of what contributes to their overall health and fulfillment will be essential. Recent research offers a valuable perspective on these evolving expectations and can help guide how providers shape their communities, services, and cultures in the years ahead.

A 2023 global survey conducted by the McKinsey Health Institute explored what "healthy aging" means to older adults, drawing responses from 21,000 individuals across 21 countries.[54] The study examined how various factors— spanning mental, physical, social, and spiritual dimensions— relate to older adults' perceptions of health and well-being.

While results varied slightly by country, several factors consistently emerged as key contributors to healthy aging. Among the 53 factors tested, those most associated with positive aging included:

- Having a sense of purpose
- Managing stress levels
- Staying mindful of posture and movement
- Engaging in continuing education
- Learning new skills
- Volunteering

Though the motivations behind these responses were diverse, the report emphasized a clear takeaway: "Providing opportunities to fulfill those motivations must be a critical priority for societies." This imperative extends to retirement communities and other senior living organizations that will need to actively support these drivers of well-being to meet the expectations of the next generation of older adults.

As senior living providers seek to support what older adults value for their health and fulfillment, it's equally essential to address the fears and concerns that often shape people's decisions about the future. According to another AP/NORC survey, some of the top concerns among older adults as they age include losing independence, affording care, becoming a burden to family, and being alone. Additional worries include insufficient planning, health and safety issues, and unmet social needs.[55]

Taken together, these two surveys provide a valuable blueprint for senior living providers: Foster communities that not only nurture the core elements of healthy aging—purpose, engagement, and lifelong learning—but also directly address the most pressing anxieties of older adults, such as loss of autonomy, financial insecurity, and loneliness.

These dual imperatives highlight a shifting expectation among older adults when it comes to senior living: They will be more drawn to environments that support both their aspirations *and* their concerns. In essence, to attract the next generation of retirees, providers must offer more than a place to live; they must provide a space to thrive. This transition involves shifting focus from the traditional reactive service and care model to a more proactive wellness and lifestyle-focused model.

Physical design

In the future, retirement communities will become increasingly diverse in design, moving away from the homogeneous models of the past. We can expect a wider variety of living options, not only across different communities but also within individual communities, offering residents more choices tailored to their lifestyle preferences.

While large, campus-style communities will remain common, we'll likely see a rise in boutique-style communities that feel more intimate and home-like, yet still offer many of the same services and amenities. For instance, many retirees today prefer to have their "own front door" rather than living in an apartment-style setting. In response, some communities may shift away from multi-story apartment buildings in favor of bungalow-style homes or quadplex units, each with its own private entrance. Even within larger CCRC campuses, we may see more "pocket neighborhood" options, featuring smaller, self-contained areas with shared common spaces, fostering a strong sense of community.

The cost structure for these smaller, community-focused models will differ from larger campus-style communities. Like the active adult apartments described in Chapter 2, the trade-off may be fewer services and amenities in exchange for an environment that promotes a neighbors-supporting-neighbors concept. Advances in technology will further enhance this model, enabling residents to receive support in ways that were previously not possible.

This trend will extend beyond independent living to include assisted living and skilled nursing providers as well. Known as the "small-house" or "greenhouse" model, this design aims to move away from the institutional, sterile atmosphere of traditional assisted living communities and nursing homes, instead creating a more nurturing, neighborly, and home-like environment. This model helps and encourages residents to have more control over their daily lives and to participate in activities of their choice, often utilizing a concierge approach.

Education and community programs

As Albert Einstein once said, "When you stop learning, you start dying." Since the last edition of this book, the focus on lifelong learning within senior living has continued to grow and prove beneficial. This is evidenced by the McKinsey survey, which revealed "formal learning/education opportunities" as one of the top four factors contributing to positive aging in older adults.

These educational programs are not only beneficial for learning and cognitive well-being, but residents also sometimes teach courses, fostering a sense of purpose in life and vocational wellness among their peers.

As part of their focus on whole-person wellness and preventative health, successful retirement communities of the future will continue to encourage and facilitate continuing education initiatives, as well as resident involvement in intergenerational programs and engagement with the wider community. These efforts may include on-site classes, resident-led workshops, and partnerships that extend beyond the community itself.

One way some communities are taking this commitment a step further is by forming partnerships with nearby universities, creating what are often referred to as university-based retirement communities (UBRCs). According to the senior living finance company Ziegler, there are around 90 CCRCs across the country that have some type of affiliation with a university.[56] In some cases, the senior living community is developed near a college campus, while in others, universities lease or sell underutilized land to senior living operators. These partnerships can significantly expand opportunities for academic engagement among residents, but they represent just one of many approaches to promoting lifelong learning in retirement. In addition to the education and lifelong learning opportunities, residents of these university-based retirement communities often enjoy the invigorating atmosphere of campus sporting events and cultural performances.

Dining

Senior living dining is evolving to reflect the changing expectations of a new generation of residents who seek more choice, flexibility, and health-conscious options. Traditional large dining halls with scheduled meals are being replaced by multiple smaller dining venues that offer a range of options, from casual cafés and pubs to fine dining. Flexible dining times offer residents greater control over their meal times, thereby enhancing their sense of independence and socialization.

An increasing number of operators are also opening their restaurants up to the public. In addition to potential new revenue, this also helps integrate senior living communities with the larger public, breaking down social barriers.

A preference toward personalized, health-focused food options continues to grow too, leading communities to reduce processed foods and embrace more fresh, local ingredients and farm-to-table approaches. Personalized menus, vegetarian and vegan meals, and even plant-based alternatives are increasingly popular, offering residents greater autonomy in tailoring their meals to suit their preferences and dietary needs. Community gardens, largely tended to by residents, are also becoming more common, fostering resident involvement and a deeper connection to the food they consume.

Technology is even playing a key role in modernizing senior living dining. From electronic menus and robotic servers to smart kitchens that streamline food preparation, these innovations improve both the dining experience and operational efficiency.

Other emerging trends, such as pop-up dining, global cuisine events, and sustainable practices like composting and reducing food waste, are further enhancing the dining experience for residents. However, senior living providers must also navigate challenges like balancing costs with quality, while ensuring consistent staff training.

Outdoor spaces

The presence of outdoor spaces in retirement communities will be increasingly sought by residents in the coming years. Research highlights the significant health benefits of spending time outdoors, particularly in environments such as parks and gardens, as well as near water. Future residents will seek these types of natural settings, even on a smaller scale, recognizing their value in promoting mental and physical well-being.

Such natural settings promote feelings of renewal, connectedness, and well-being. Research shows that older adults who regularly spend time outside often experience reduced symptoms of depression and anxiety as the calming effects of nature boost mood and happiness. Outdoor physical activities, such as walking or biking in natural environments, offer even more mental health benefits than indoor exercises, including improved energy and mental focus. Therefore, communal amenities such as walking paths, nature trails, mini-parks, and even adult playgrounds will become more common.

Along with enhancing mental health, outdoor spaces help reduce feelings of isolation by encouraging social interactions. Older adults who spend time outdoors in community settings tend to feel more connected, which in turn supports their emotional and spiritual well-being. Access to green spaces has also been linked to lower risks of early death and a reduction in diseases such as cancer, lung disease, and kidney disease.

While residents highly value outdoor spaces and have been shown to positively impact health and well-being, retirement community developers must be intentional—and often creative—in how they design and utilize these areas. Ample outdoor spaces can be challenging to justify financially, particularly if they do not directly contribute to revenue or end up being underutilized. The goal should be to create outdoor environments that are not only inviting and beneficial to residents but also practical and sustainable from a development perspective.

Technology

Long gone are the days when older adults, for the most part, were not online. According to Pew Research, approximately 88% of Americans over age 65 are now online, a number that is increasing each year.[57] (This is up from 60% at the time of the last edition of this book in 2016 and up from 73% in 2019, just before the COVID-19 pandemic, which necessitated the need for many older adults to go online for video conferencing.)

The conversation is no longer about whether a retirement community should have Wi-Fi throughout its premises. This is now expected as a bare minimum. The conversation around technology in senior living today is increasingly focused on various aspects, including social engagement technology, virtual reality, artificial intelligence/robots, digital communication platforms, telehealth, predictive analytics, and more. While many of these technology solutions will also be available to people in their own homes, the most forward-thinking retirement communities will integrate them into every aspect of the community to nurture connectedness, enhance operational efficiency and service delivery, streamline communication, support resident care and well-being, and ultimately elevate the resident experience.

Although we are just now on the brink of many technological breakthroughs, particularly in the realm of artificial intelligence (AI), there is no doubt that technology will transform how senior living providers address the numerous challenges posed by a rapidly growing senior population.

Consider, for example, smart home technology that utilizes remote monitoring. A remote home monitoring system can detect subtle shifts in an older adult's health and movement behaviors. Equipped with Wi-Fi-enabled motion sensors, door sensors, and sometimes cameras, these in-home systems gather data on the resident's daily activity patterns and will provide alerts to the staff or care team about any notable changes or potential emergencies. While reluctance to in-home monitoring may still hinder adoption for some residents and consumers, increasing comfort with technology is gradually easing these concerns. As consumers become increasingly accustomed to technological advancements, particularly those that promote safety and independence, the acceptance of these systems will continue to accelerate.

Additionally, telehealth services and care coordination will be powered by AI and video to enable easier physician consultation and coordination among community staff, families, and caregivers. In the not-too-distant future, senior living communities will likely utilize AI-enabled robots to provide everything from physical assistance to answering health-related questions and offering companionship.

Another area where technology usage is rapidly increasing within senior living is with resident engagement software. This software helps residents foster connections and learn more about one another, thereby reducing loneliness, while also offering accessible programming. These solutions empower residents by allowing them to better manage their own activity schedules, coordinate transportation, submit work requests, and more easily connect with other residents who share their interests. This is also beneficial to the management team, as it provides valuable insights into program usage and resident preferences, making it easier to track which activities and offerings are most popular. Furthermore, such data helps refine community programs to better align with resident needs and enhance overall satisfaction.

This type of resident engagement software can also be highly beneficial to residents with limited mobility or other physical impairments, who may not be able to participate as actively in on-site events and activities. Advancements in engagement technology enable meaningful interaction across distances and cater to diverse physical and sensory abilities. Modern platforms deliver programming directly to resident rooms through apps or streaming services, which even family members can join. With adaptable features, these tools support residents with sight, hearing, or mobility challenges, offering a more personalized and person-centered approach.

Virtual reality is yet another innovative technology that is rapidly being adopted among senior living providers and residents. Virtual reality offers a transformative way for residents to connect, reminisce, and explore. With applications tailored for personalized memory journeys, older adults can revisit meaningful places from their past, such as the city where they were born or their favorite vacation spots, bringing comfort and joy through immersive reminiscence therapy. This can be highly stimulating mentally and emotionally, positively impacting one's overall well-being.

Reminiscence therapy via virtual reality has shown itself to be particularly effective for those with memory-related illnesses. But perhaps most powerful, virtual reality fosters new friendships and shared experiences among residents, bringing them together to create memorable moments and stories that are cherished by both residents and their families.

Lastly, there may not be any area where technology will have a greater impact in senior living than in supportive living and care delivery. Predictive data—the process of analyzing large amounts of information computationally for trends, patterns, and associations—is rapidly entering the senior living industry and is expected to further accelerate with the evolution of artificial intelligence.

For example, data generated from remote sensor patterns, combined with remote wellness monitors that track vital signs or glucose levels in diabetics, can help staff at a retirement community predict when a resident might be at higher risk of a health event or hospitalization. The capacity of computers to continuously track such data can also help prevent illness or unnecessary health deterioration, enabling residents to remain independent for longer.

There's little doubt that advancements in technology, science, and medicine will transform the experience of aging in ways we can scarcely imagine today. These innovations will impact older adults regardless of where they reside—whether aging in place at home or in a retirement community. In the near term, however, retirement communities and other senior living providers may be more likely than individual older adults to have the infrastructure, trained staff, and financial resources needed to implement and support the more advanced and costly technologies.

Resident engagement and empowerment

As mentioned earlier in this chapter, the future of senior living will not (and should not) be focused purely on physical design and technology aspects. Perhaps most important is how the community makes residents *feel*. The next generation of retirees wants their voices to be heard. In general, they do not want to be told how to live or be subject to a rigid schedule. This would go against the independence this generation longs to maintain.

To thrive, the senior living industry must view residents not as passive recipients but as active partners in shaping better, more responsive communities. The most successful communities of the future will foster active resident councils and create regular opportunities for dialogue between leadership and residents—especially in CCRCs, where residents have made a substantial financial investment. Rather than simply offering staff-led activities, communities will empower residents to be actively involved in planning and executing events, providing resources and support as necessary.

It's true that genuinely engaging residents may require more time and effort, from gathering input to thoughtfully balancing diverse perspectives and responding promptly. Residents also have a responsibility to be respectful and empathetic towards the many priorities that the leadership team may be juggling at any given time. But this investment in residents can lead to more informed decisions, stronger trust, and a healthier community culture. With a straightforward and efficient process in place, involving residents becomes not just manageable but also strategically wise.

While not every suggestion or idea can be implemented, every voice should be welcomed with respect. Residents deserve to be treated as guests, clients, and stakeholders because in truth, they are all three. No matter how nice a community may be, if residents do not feel respected for who they are and what they can contribute, it will ultimately be detrimental to the community. While residents should be the best referral source, those who feel dismissed will not be motivated to encourage others to move in.

Fostering engagement among residents also has a positive impact on their overall well-being. When residents are empowered to make decisions and are engaged in the community in a meaningful and personal way, it decreases loneliness, prolongs their independence, and improves their overall well-being. Ultimately, this offers senior living providers the opportunity to experience improved long-term clinical and financial outcomes.

Resident empowerment and engagement do not end with independent living; it's also critical for residents who are receiving care. The concept of "person-centered care" prioritizes the unique preferences, values, and interests of each individual, encouraging residents and their families to take an active role in their care. This model involves collaboration among the entire care team—including family members—ensuring that loved ones' likes and dislikes are understood and respected. This means residents are viewed as partners who, whenever possible, play an important role in planning, developing, and monitoring care services, rather than as a passive recipient of services.

In assisted living communities, for example, person-centered care is often reflected in personalized activities, meal choices, and meaningful interactions with staff, all designed to honor and enhance each resident's daily experiences.

Again, it is essential to remember that this doesn't always guarantee that a resident's care wishes will be met. For the safety of the resident and those around them, staff may make decisions that are met with resistance from the resident. Ultimately, person-centered care is about showing compassion and respect for the resident each step of the way, and trying as best as possible to meet a resident's wishes, while also recognizing that every decision or recommendation may not be exactly what the resident would want, especially when the safety of the resident or those around them could be at risk.

Communities that embrace a "person-centered" approach to care will, in turn, be more embraced by their target market because residents and their families will feel respected and cared for as individuals.

Evolving models of affordability

This is an interesting time for the senior living industry, as demand for high-end, luxurious senior living is at an all-time high, with no signs of slowing down. At the same time, the National Council on Aging reports that more than 17 million older adults age 65-plus are economically insecure, with incomes below 200% of the federal poverty level, many of whom may financially qualify for government-supported affordable housing.[56]

Of course, those in the middle—sometimes referred to as the "missing middle"—are often overlooked when it comes to the availability of senior housing. This is because they do not have the financial means to afford the high-end senior living options, but they also do not qualify for government-supported affordable housing.

Let's look at each of these categories separately, beginning with the two extremes.

Luxury senior housing

According to a 2022 Pew Research Center analysis, adults age 65 and above have made the most notable progress up the income ladder in recent decades.[58] The Baby Boomer generation (born 1946 to 1964) represents nearly 20% of the U.S. population, but currently holds the most wealth in the United States, accounting for over 51% of total household wealth.[59] The concentration of wealth among this age cohort mirrors that of the United States as a whole, where 1% of households own approximately 30% of the wealth.[60]

This prosperity is attributable to several factors, including savvy 401(k) investing, pensions, inheritance, and an increasing number of college-educated retirees who earn higher wages during their working years.

This upward financial shift for retirees is a key driver of the growing demand for luxury senior living. The demand encompasses everything from white-glove concierge services and lavish grounds to indulgent spas and five-star dining, much like what you might experience at some of the finest hotels or resorts.

The luxury senior living market is evolving to meet the changing preferences of today's affluent retirees. Increasingly, the focus is shifting from traditional notions of luxury to an emphasis on personalization and creating a sense of indulgence. Operators are redefining luxury as an experience—a "vibe"—that makes residents feel truly special. Inspired by world-renowned organizations like The Ritz-Carlton and even Disney, communities are training staff at all levels to deliver elevated, tailored service that goes beyond excellence.

These communities also offer unique, resident-specific experiences, such as gourmet wine dinners, beekeeping classes, and curated cultural events. The physical spaces also reflect the high aesthetic expectations of their residents, featuring elegant designs and premium materials that rival the sophistication of luxury homes and iconic global destinations. By combining exquisite environments with personalized service, these communities aim to create a distinctive lifestyle that resonates with retirees accustomed to the finer things in life.

Affordable senior housing

While the senior living industry focuses on meeting the rising demand for high-end communities, it must not overlook a parallel and urgent reality: The number of low-income older adults in the U.S. is steadily increasing, and so is the need for more affordable housing.

In this context, "affordable" senior housing refers primarily to rent-subsidized programs offered through government agencies like the U.S.

Department of Housing and Urban Development (HUD). Eligibility for HUD financing is typically based on household income being at or below 80% of the area's median family income, calculated using a family-of-four benchmark. Income thresholds are adjusted based on household size, with those well below the 80% threshold qualifying for higher levels of subsidy.

As of 2023, approximately 5.1 million subsidized housing units in the U.S. were occupied by people of all ages, making up about 10% of the rental housing market.[61] Of these, roughly 1.9 million, or 37%, were occupied by adults age 62 and older who benefit from HUD's rental assistance programs. Yet, there are still millions of older adults who qualify for aid but are left without access due to a lack of vacant units.

For many in this lower-income demographic, additional support comes from state and local programs, often through means-tested services such as Medicaid, which can provide housing and care services in select settings. Again, keep in mind that recent federal budget changes have resulted in significant Medicaid cuts, which may lead to tightened eligibility requirements or reduced benefits in some states, potentially limiting access to these critical services.

Governments at all levels have begun to respond to this growing housing need by preserving existing affordable housing stock and encouraging the development of new units. Local initiatives such as tax abatements, zoning adjustments, and public-private partnerships are helping to incentivize developers to build for low-income older adults. Mixed-income communities and low-income housing tax credit (LIHTC) projects have made a positive impact, but current efforts still fall short of meeting the full scale of demand.

While the lowest-income older adults face the most urgent challenges, they are not alone; a broader group of older adults is also increasingly vulnerable to housing instability. There are more than 17 million Americans age 65-

plus who are economically insecure, generally defined as living at or below 200% of the federal poverty level (FPL). Many people in this group will likely struggle in the years to come. As stated in a 2025 Urban Institute article, "Today, senior households—many of whom are on fixed incomes—are facing a combined crisis of housing affordability, accessibility, and availability. As the country's population ages, policymakers must prioritize solutions for older adults in the housing crisis. Without action, the consequences will be severe."[63]

The reality is clear: Many older adults cannot afford to age in place, and without sufficient affordable alternatives, they face housing insecurity in their most vulnerable years. Despite some progress, the supply of affordable senior housing is far from adequate, leaving millions of qualified individuals unserved. Without stronger investment and more deliberate policy action, the shortage will continue to worsen, leading to greater instability, increased reliance on public programs, and diminished quality of life for many older adults. Addressing the affordable housing gap isn't just a matter of infrastructure; it's a matter of dignity, equity, and public responsibility. It also presents a big opportunity for the future of senior living.

Middle-market senior living

While senior living solutions evolve to serve both high-income individuals and those qualifying for subsidized support, a rapidly growing segment remains underserved: middle-income older adults who fall between these two ends of the financial spectrum.

The Urban Institute projects that the number of middle-income older adults (those not poor enough for Medicaid but not wealthy enough to pay out of pocket for care or housing) will double by 2033, with many still lacking sufficient assets to cover housing and healthcare.[64]

A big challenge and opportunity for the senior living industry is to offer more options that are appropriately priced for these middle-income older adults. In recent years, the industry has placed increasing attention on developing housing options for this demographic, particularly through models like active adult apartments and rental retirement communities, as outlined in Chapter 2. Rather than focusing solely on high-end amenities, many of these more moderately priced communities are shifting their emphasis toward delivering a high-quality resident experience, often by streamlining luxury features in favor of affordability and livability.

For instance, instead of spending money on lavish spas, pools, and fitness centers, providers will contract with local organizations and clubs offering these amenities and provide regular transportation to and from each location. New CCRCs may even forgo building their own healthcare center, instead choosing to locate near an existing healthcare facility and establishing a contractual partnership. The savings generated from these types of development decisions can be passed on to the residents in the form of lower fees.

Housing for middle-market older adults can also be achieved by combining highly efficient planning and project management. For instance, using alternate building materials no longer necessarily translates to lower quality. Lower-cost materials include natural and more durable materials that increase sustainability and reduce long-term maintenance costs. Low-cost development may also include using locally sourced building materials, which eliminates higher transportation costs for materials. Of course, these initiatives have a double impact: not only do they help the environment by reducing the consumption of non-renewable resources and minimizing waste, but they also bring us to the next future trend in senior living...

Environmental sustainability

Anecdotal evidence suggests that while residents currently living in retirement communities have been somewhat indifferent towards environmental sustainability, this is starting to shift, especially for those in more progressive regions of the country. Not only is it changing for residents, but a growing number of senior living developers are seeing the benefits of sustainable building.

Reflecting a trend in recent years in the residential building sector, we'll continue to see an increase in the number of Leadership in Energy and Environmental Design (LEED)-certified retirement communities, which focus on energy, space, and water efficiency, as well as reducing waste and using environmentally friendly building materials. This will likely evolve to also include features such as solar energy, rainwater harvesting, low-flow water fixtures, recycled construction materials, daylight harvesting, high-efficiency lighting fixtures, and more. Although some providers may not apply for LEED certification, they will still implement many of the same cost-saving sustainability features.

To help reduce a retirement community's carbon footprint, walkability and access to transportation will also be a growing focus. Although the price of urban-located land can be an obstacle, many new communities will look to build or repurpose buildings in urban areas so residents can walk or have easy access to stores, restaurants, and entertainment centers. Of course, this provides a secondary benefit to residents by increasing their level of activity and social interactions—a feeling of being a part of the broader community rather than being cut off from it.

Communities with an environmental focus will also provide educational programs on sustainability topics, empowering residents to help make an impact. Some communities will even provide residents with updates on their month-to-month energy savings or the pounds of compost collected, so that the entire resident population has a sense of buy-in. This, too, has a secondary benefit of providing residents with a common focus and a reason for increased interactions.

Affinity communities

Affinity communities, which are meant to cultivate social connections among those who share similar interests and lifestyles, are not new to retirement housing. Early church-sponsored CCRCs provided an affinity community of people with similar religious beliefs.

Today, new models for affinity housing are emerging in response to changing needs and new concepts. In addition to faith-sponsored affinity communities, a 2024 blog post on myLifeSite.net highlights various examples of existing affinity communities including artists, military, equestrian, golf, Zen and meditation, lifelong learning/university-based retirement communities (UBRCs), and even Jimmy Buffett-inspired Margaritaville communities.[65]

One type of affinity community that is growing—albeit much slower than many would like—is LGBTQ+-focused communities. While LGBTQ+ older adults share the same age-related concerns as any older adult, including eventually being dependent on others for daily living assistance and care, they may continue to struggle with a society that often lacks the knowledge and/or appreciation of their special needs.

For instance, LGBTQ+ older adults may face significant challenges in accessing care, including hesitancy to seek certain health services, reluctance to disclose their sexual identity due to fear of discrimination or being stigmatized, and higher risks of depression, suicide, and substance abuse. They also report greater feelings of isolation.

As described in a 2024 AARP article, LGBTQ+ retirement communities have historically fallen under the affordable living category. They are often developed by nonprofit organizations that offer community-based activities and social services such as health and wellness education, support groups, and food and transportation assistance. However, the article notes that "LGBTQ+ retirement communities have broadened into different shapes and sizes that echo developments in the mainstream active-adult market." [66]

Healthcare

As part of the Affordable Care Act (ACA) of 2010, the Centers for Medicare & Medicaid Services (CMS) established the CMS Innovation Center to explore new healthcare payment and delivery models aimed at improving care quality while reducing costs, particularly for older adults. One of its primary initiatives has been the promotion of accountable care organizations (ACOs), which are networks of healthcare providers—including doctors, hospitals, and post-acute care providers—who collaborate to deliver coordinated, high-quality care to Medicare patients.

By aligning payment with outcomes, ACOs incentivize healthcare providers to emphasize preventive care, reduce redundancies, and improve communication across care teams. Instead of being paid based on the volume of services delivered, participating providers share in the savings they generate when they deliver high-quality, cost-efficient care. This shared savings model rewards organizations that meet specific benchmarks for patient outcomes, care coordination, and cost control, thereby encouraging a more holistic, proactive approach to healthcare.

In previous editions of this book, we examined how some CCRCs and senior living providers began exploring ACO participation to improve care coordination and outcomes. In recent years, this interest has grown as senior living organizations increasingly seek to position themselves as integral players within the broader continuum of care, working alongside hospitals, primary care providers, and post-acute services. By integrating more closely with healthcare systems and data-sharing networks, these communities aim to support better health outcomes for their residents, reduce unnecessary hospitalizations, and demonstrate their value as proactive partners in population health management.

While ACOs remain an important vehicle for these efforts, they now represent just one of several models under the broader umbrella of value-based care, a healthcare delivery approach that shifts the focus from the volume of services provided to the quality and outcomes of care delivered.

Today, value-based care has become a central strategy across the senior living industry, with providers embracing a range of innovative models to prioritize resident well-being, preventive health, and holistic support. These approaches may include solutions such as on-site primary care clinics, predictive health technologies, wellness programs, and partnerships with Medicare Advantage plans and third-party care providers.

This shift is being fueled by evolving resident expectations, regulatory pressures, and the need to manage rising healthcare costs while enhancing residents' quality of life. As a result, value-based care in senior living now encompasses not only ACOs but also a growing array of risk-sharing partnerships, data-driven care coordination efforts, and condition-specific initiatives.

Conclusions

Each generation builds on the successful models of the past to formulate new concepts that advance our human experience. Nowhere is this truer than in concepts for senior living. With innovation around physical design, service offerings, and technology in senior living, the industry has come a long way from the indigents' old age homes and hospital wards of a past era.

Aging is inevitable. Your ability to remain able-bodied and independent throughout your lifetime is uncertain. However, your future care and comfort can be more secure with proper planning and guidance. By educating yourself on the options described in this book, and by taking into consideration your personal circumstances, preferences, and objectives, you can begin to chart the best course for your future so that you and your family can approach your later years with more confidence and peace of mind.

Unlike in the family-centric agrarian societies of the past, families in our modern industrialized society often live far apart. In those days, parents expected their children to provide for them in the future. Today, it's common for parents to provide for their own future needs and to spare their children from that burden. It's not that families are less intimate. Parents still love their children, and children still revere their parents, but the advent of new living models, such as full-care CCRCs, makes it increasingly possible for parents to provide for themselves, and many prefer to do so.

Additionally, dual-income families are much more common than in the past. Approximately 60% of two-parent households now have both parents earning an income,[67] and within these households, 45% have parents who both work full-time—an increase from just 31% in the 1970s.[68][69] As a result, adult children are less likely to have the flexibility to care for aging parents, since their work commitments have increased.

Changing Family Dynamics and Solo Aging

As outlined in the Introduction, a significant shift is occurring in the availability of family members to provide care for aging relatives. Today, more solo-agers than ever before are reaching their later years without a spouse or immediate family members nearby to assist with daily needs and long-term care. This trend is compounded by the sharp decline in the number of adult children who are able or available to arrange, coordinate, or personally provide care for their aging parents. As family sizes decrease and geographical distances grow, the traditional model of relying on close relatives for support is becoming less feasible for many.

The Shift Toward Independence in Senior Living

The major driving force is not so much the adult children's inability to care for their aging parents, whether due to limited time, lack of expertise, geographic distance, or the emotional and physical toll. Instead, many older adults today actively choose a different path. They value their independence and take proactive steps to manage their own well-being, seeking professional and expert care through their own arrangements rather than relying on their children. For some, there is comfort and satisfaction in knowing they will not become a burden to their loved ones. This sense of autonomy allows families to remain close and supportive, while also celebrating the financial independence and self-reliance that both generations have achieved.

The societal changes that have unfolded over recent decades, along with reductions in government support programs—particularly those affecting lower-income seniors—underscore the growing importance of personal planning for retirement and future living arrangements. In this evolving landscape, taking responsibility for one's own future is more critical than ever.

If you are in your mid-retirement years, NOW is the time to begin planning. If you have adult children, consider having an open and honest discussion with them about your housing and care preferences for the later stages of life. If you wish to remain in your home, carefully consider each of the implications outlined in Chapter 1. Consider not only your current lifestyle, but also the potential needs that may arise in the future. If you determine that staying in your home is impractical, either due to the lack of a family caregiver or for other reasons, then you need to consider the alternatives described in this book.

Some impractical aspects of aging at home could be addressed by downsizing or moving to an active adult community or senior living co-op. Yet, these options do not provide the type of healthcare services you may eventually require. If you prefer to live in a location that offers limited care services, an independent living community may be a suitable option. Alternatively, as described in Chapter 3, some individuals find peace of mind living in a retirement community that offers a full continuum of care, although such communities often require a substantial financial commitment, which may not be feasible for everyone.

For more information to help you make the choice that is best for you, please see the Resources section provided at the back of this book.

Congratulations on taking the first steps in planning for your future housing and healthcare needs!

Resources

- *my*LifeSite: mylifesite.net
- Genworth/CareScout Cost of Care Survey: carescout.com/cost-of-care
- AARP Long Term Care Scoresheet by State: ltsschoices.aarp.org/scorecard-report/2023
- American Seniors Housing Association: ashaliving.org/
- LeadingAge: leadingage.org
- Senior Cooperative Housing: seniorcoopliving.org/
- NIC: nic.org
- American Association for Long Term Care Insurance: aaltci.org
- CARF Consumer Guide to Life Plan Communities: Quality and Financial Viability:
- carf.org/resources/public/
- Propublica Non-Profit Explorer: projects.propublica.org/nonprofits/
- National Continuing Care Residents Association (NaCCRA): naccra.com
- Naturally Occurring Retirement Communities (NORCS): norcs.org/
- U.S. Dept. of Veterans Affairs- LTC benefits: va.gov/geriatrics/guide/longtermcare/
- U.S. Dept. of Health and Human Services: acl.gov/ltc
- National Center for Health Statistics: cdc.gov/nchs/

- Village to Village Network: vtvnetwork.org/
- Federal Long-Term Care Partnership Program: ltcfeds.gov/
- AARP Caregiving Resource Center: aarp.org/home-family/caregiving/
- National Alliance for Caregiving: caregiving.org/
- National Care Planning Council: https: longtermcarelink.net/
- National PACE Association: npaonline.org/
- Where You Live Matters: whereyoulivematters.org/
- Long Term Care Ombudsman: ltcombudsman.org/
- FTC Consumer Advice on Reverse Mortgages: consumer.ftc.gov/articles/reverse-mortgages
- Tax Foundation- Tax Statistics: taxfoundation.org/

Works Cited

1. Pew Research Center. "Population Change in the U.S. and the World from 1950 to 2050." 30 Jan. 2014, www.pewresearch.org.
2. United States Census Bureau. "2010 Census Shows 65 and Older Population Growing Faster than Total U.S. Population." 30 Nov. 2011, www.census.gov/newsroom/releases/archives/2010_census/cb11-cn192.html.
3. United States Census Bureau. "Older People and Aging: 2020 Census Shows 1 in 6 People in the United States Were 65 and Over." 25 May 2023, www.census.gov.
4. Administration for Community Living. "2020 Profile of Older Americans." May 2021, www.acl.gov.
5. AARP. "Age 65+ Adults Are Projected to Outnumber Children by 2023." 14 Mar. 2018, www.aarp.org.
6. "Annual global life expectancy at select ages 1950-2100." *Statista*, 2024, www.statista.com/statistics/1460165/global-life-expectancy-by-age-historical/. Accessed 9 Aug. 2025.
7. AARP. "The Aging of the Baby Boom and the Growing Care Gap." Aug. 2013, www.aarp.org.
8. Joint Center for Housing Studies of Harvard University. "The Number of People Living Alone in Their 80s and 90s is Set to Soar." www.jchs.harvard.edu.
9. American Association for Long-Term Care Insurance. "New Report Reveals Ages When Claims Begin for Long-Term Care Insurance." 2024, www.aaLTCI.org.
10. Farrell, Chris. "House Payments that Don't Retire." *Next Avenue*, 9 June 2025, www.nextavenue.org/house-payments-that-dont-retire/[2].

11. Ramsey Solutions. "How to Keep 3 Common Home Repairs from Busting Your Budget." "Ramsey Solutions", 28 Feb. 2025, www.ramseysolutions.com/budgeting/keep-home-repairs-from-busting-budget.

12. NCH Stats. "Average Home Value Increase Per Year in the US." *NCH Stats*, 2025, https://nchstats.com/average-home-value-increase-us/. Accessed 12 Sept. 2025.

13. U.S. News. "How Much Should You Spend on Aging in Place Renovations? Retirees Weigh In." "U.S. News & World Report", 12 July 2025, money.usnews.com/money/retirement/articles/how-much-should-you-spend-on-aging-in-place-renovations-retirees-weigh-in.

14. Genworth/CareScout Financial. "Calculate the Cost of Long-Term Care Near You." www.carescout.com/cost-of-care.

15. National Institute on Aging. "Social Isolation, Loneliness in Older People Pose Health Risks." "National Institute on Aging", 23 Apr. 2019, www.nia.nih.gov/news/social-isolation-loneliness-older-people-pose-health-risks.

16. AARP. "New AARP Report Finds Family Caregivers Provide $600 Billion in Unpaid Care Across the U.S." 8 Mar. 2023, www.aarp.org/caregiving/financial-legal/info-2023/unpaid-caregivers-provide-billions-in-care.html.

17. AARP. "More Than 60% Say Caregiving Increased Their Level of Stress and Worry, New AARP Report Finds." 1 Nov. 2023, www.aarp.org/caregiving/health/info-2023/report-caregiver-mental-health.html.

18. Family Caregiver Alliance. "Caregiver Statistics: Health, Technology, and Caregiving Resources." Family Caregiver Alliance, 2023, https://www.caregiver.org/resource/caregiver-statistics-health-technology-and-caregiving-resources/.

19. JBS International. "Family Caregiving: Mental & Physical Health Effects." JBS International, 29 Nov. 2024, www.jbsinternational.com/blog/family-caregiving-mental-physical-health-effects. Accessed 29 July 2025.

20. Family Caregiver Alliance. "Caregiver Health." Family Caregiver Alliance, 14 July 2021, www.caregiver.org/resource/caregiver-health/. Accessed 29 July 2025.
21. National Alliance for Caregiving and MetLife Mature Market Institute. *The MetLife Caregiving Cost Study: Productivity Losses to U.S. Business.* July 2006, https://www.kff.org/wp-content/uploads/sites/2/2010/09/caregiver_cost_study.pdf.
22. AARP. "Family Caregivers Spend More Than $7,200 a Year on Out-of-Pocket Costs." 29 June 2021, www.aarp.org/caregiving/financial-legal/info-2021/high-out-of-pocket-costs.html.
23. Home Care Association of America and National Association for Home Care and Hospice. "The Home Care Workforce Crisis: An Industry Report and Call to Action." Mar. 2023, www.hcaoa.org/uploads/1/3/3/0/133041104/workforce_report_and_call_to_action_final_03272023.pdf.
24. The Commonwealth Fund. "Addressing the Shortage of Direct Care Workers: Insights from Seven States." 19 Mar. 2024, www.commonwealthfund.org/publications/issue-briefs/2024/mar/addressing-shortage-direct-care-workers-insights-seven-states.
25. Centers for Medicare and Medicaid Services. "Skilled Nursing Facility Care." Medicare.gov.
26. Pitturo, Marlene. "NORCs: Some of the Best Retirement Communities Occur Naturally." "Next Avenue", 7 May 2012, www.nextavenue.org/norcs-some-best-retirement-communities-occur-naturally/.
27. Joint Center for Housing Studies of Harvard University. "Naturally Occurring Retirement Communities Are Common in Metros in Florida, Arizona, and Oregon." 5 Jan. 2021, www.jchs.harvard.edu/blog/naturally-occurring-retirement-communities-score-lower-livability.
28. Greenfield, Emily, et al. "A Tale of Two Community Initiatives for Promoting Aging in Place." "The Gerontologist", vol. 53, no. 6, 2013, pp. 928–938, academic.oup.com/gerontologist/article/53/6/928/636231.

29. Senior Cooperative Foundation. "Senior Housing Cooperatives." www.seniorcoops.org.
30. Harvard Health Publishing. "Why Life Expectancy in the US Is Falling." 20 Oct. 2022, www.health.harvard.edu/blog/why-life-expectancy-in-the-us-is-falling-202210202835.
31. North Carolina Department of Insurance. "CCRC Reference Guide and Listing." www.ncdoi.gov/licensees/continuing-care-retirement-communities-ccrc/ccrc-reference-guide-and-listing.
32. Virginia State Corporation Commission. "Guide to the Regulation of Continuing Care Retirement Communities." www.scc.virginia.gov/consumers/insurance/health-insurance-consumer/tips,-guides-publications/regulation-of-continuing-care-retirement-communiti/.
33. California Department of Social Services. "Resources for Residents and Families." www.cdss.ca.gov/inforesources/community-care/continuing-care/resources-for-residents-and-families.
34. Nelson, Mary Kate. "Only 22% of CCRCs in the U.S. are For-Profit." Senior Housing News, 24 May 2018, https://seniorhousingnews.com/2018/05/24/only-22-of-ccrcs-in-the-u-s-are-for-profit/.
35. Moeller, Philip. "Aging Insights: Residents Share What It's Like to Live in a Retirement Community." "U.S. News & World Report", 20 Aug. 2013, money.usnews.com/money/blogs/the-best-life/2013/08/20/aging-insights-residents-share-what-its-like-to-live-in-a-retirement-community.
36. International Council on Active Aging. "ICAA/ProMatura Wellness Benchmarks: The National Benchmarks Report." 2017, www.icaa.cc/business/benchmarks.htm.
37. National Investment Center for Seniors Housing & Care. "Research Shows Senior Living Communities Promote Wellness and Healthy Aging." 18 June 2024, www.nic.org/resources/research-shows-senior-living-communities-promote-wellness-and-healthy-aging/.

38. Winklevoss, Howard E., and Alton Alwyn V. Powell. "Continuing Care Retirement Communities: An Empirical, Financial and Legal Analysis." 1984.
39. Maag, Stephen. "CCRC Without Walls: Care Models of the Future." LeadingAge, 2012.
40. Eckhouse, Brian. "Americans Risk Losing Life Savings When Retirement Homes Go Bust." "Bloomberg", 3 Dec. 2025, www.bloomberg.com/news/features/2024-12-03/americans-risk-losing-life-savings-when-retirement-homes-go-bust.
41. National Investment Center for Seniors Housing & Care. "CCRC Performance 1Q2025: A Deep Dive into Entrance Fee vs. Rental CCRC Trends." *NIC Nots Blog.* 19 May 2025. https://www.nic.org/blog/ccrc-performance-1q-2025-a-deep-dive-into-entrance-fee-vs-rental-ccrc-trends/.
42. National Investment Center for Seniors Housing & Care. "Seniors Housing Occupancy Rate Drops Below 88% in Second Quarter." *NIC News & Press.* 12 July 2018. https://www.nic.org/news-press/seniors-housing-occupancy-rate-drops-below-88-in-second-quarter/.
43. Stulick, Amy. "'SNF-Heavy' CCRCs Continue to Suffer as Staffing, Revenue Pressures Mount." "Skilled Nursing News", 10 Apr. 2024, skillednursingnews.com/2024/04/snf-heavy-ccrcs-continue-to-suffer-as-staffing-revenue-pressures-mount/.
44. Kemper, Peter, et al. "Long-Term Care over an Uncertain Future: What Can Current Retirees Expect?" "INQUIRY: The Journal of Health Care Organization, Provision, and Financing", vol. 42, no. 4, Nov. 2005, journals.sagepub.com/doi/abs/10.5034/inquiryjrnl_42.4.335.
45. Office of the Assistant Secretary for Planning and Evaluation. "What Is the Lifetime Risk of Needing and Receiving Long-Term Services and Supports?" Apr. 2019.
46. Chen, Anqi, Alicia H. Munnell, and Nilufer Gok. "Do Households Have a Good Sense of Their Long-Term Care Risks?" Center for Retirement Research at Boston College, Working Paper 2025-5, Feb. 2025.

47. American Association for Long-Term Care Insurance. "What Is the Probability You'll Need Long-Term Care?" www.aaLTCI.org/long-term-care-insurance/learning-center/probability-long-term-care.php.
48. Administration for Community Living. "How Much Care Will You Need?" www.acl.gov/ltc/basic-needs/how-much-care-will-you-need.
49. American Health Care Association and National Center for Assisted Living. "Comments on Medicare Program: Prospective Payment System and Consolidated Billing for Skilled Nursing Facilities; Updates to Quality Reporting Program and Value-Based Purchasing Program for Fiscal Year 2025." 28 May 2024, https://www.ahcancal.org/News-and-Communications/Fact-Sheets/Letters/CMS-1802-P_FY%202025%20SNF%20PPS_AHCA_NCAL%20Comments_Appendix_05.28.2024.pdf.
50. Tompson, T., et al. "Long-Term Care: Perceptions, Experiences, and Attitudes Among Americans 40 and Older." AP-NORC, 2013, www.apnorc.org/PDFs/Long%20Term%20Care/AP_NORC_Long%20Term%20Care%20Perception_FINAL%20REPORT.pdf.
51. Bankers Life. "What's the Difference Between Medicare and Long-Term Care Insurance?" www.bankerslife.com/insights/understanding-insurance/long-term-care-insurance-versus-medicare-whats-the-difference/.
52. Kaiser Family Foundation. "Status of State Medicaid Expansion Decisions." Kaiser Family Foundation, 9 May 2025, https://www.kff.org/status-of-state-medicaid-expansion-decisions/.
53. NIC MAPs. "Senior Housing Industry Forecast: What to Expect in 2025 and Beyond." NIC MAPs Blog, 2025, www.nicmap.com/blog/senior-housing-industry-forecast-what-to-expect-in-2025-and-beyond/.
54. McKinsey Health Institute. "Age Is Just a Number: How Older Adults View Healthy Aging." 22 May 2023, www.mckinsey.com/mhi/our-insights/age-is-just-a-number-how-older-adults-view-healthy-aging.
55. Foresight 50+ by AARP and NORC. "More Than Money: How Loneliness and Isolation Color Older Adults' Concerns About Aging." NORC at the University of Chicago, March

56. 2025, https://www.norc.org/research/library/how-loneliness-isolation-color-older-adults-concerns-about-aging.html.
56. Ziegler Investment Banking. Senior Living Finance Z-News. B.C. Ziegler and Company, 4 Dec. 2023, https://www.ziegler.com/media/la2p5mak/sl_znews_120423.pdf.
57. Pew Research Center. "Internet and Technology Use Among Older Adults." *Pew Research Center*, 2024, https://www.pewresearch.org/internet/fact-sheet/internet-broadband/. Accessed 12 Sept. 2025.
58. Pew Research Center. "Older Workers Are Growing in Number and Earning Higher Wages." *Pew Research Center*, 13 Dec. 2023, https://www.pewresearch.org/social-trends/2023/12/14/older-workers-are-growing-in-number-and-earning-higher-wages/. Accessed 12 Sept. 2025.
59. Author Unknown. "Boomers Are the Wealthiest Generation Ever Lived." *Yahoo Finance*, 12 Sept. 2025, finance.yahoo.com/news/boomers-wealthiest-generation-ever-lived-104103574.html.
60. Roberts, Hal. "Who Are the Top One Percent by Income or Net Worth in 2025?" *Don't Quit Your Day Job*, 31 Dec. 2024, dqydj.com/top-one-percent-united-states/. Accessed 12 Sept. 2025.
61. United States, Department of Housing and Urban Development. Worst Case Housing Needs: 2023 Report to Congress. U.S. Department of Housing and Urban Development, 2023, https://www.huduser.gov/portal/portal/sites/default/files/pdf/Worst-Case-Housing-Needs-2023.pdf. Accessed 12 Sept. 2025.
62. National Council on Aging. "Get the Facts on Economic Security for Seniors." National Council on Aging, 1 June 2024, https://www.ncoa.org/article/get-the-facts-on-economic-security-for-seniors/.
63. Urban Institute. "America's Housing Market Is Failing Older Adults." *Urban Institute*, 11 Mar. 2025, https://www.urban.org/urban-

64. wire/americas-housing-market-failing-older-adults. Accessed 12 Sept. 2025.
65. Urban Institute. "Middle-Income Seniors Face a Gap in Housing and Health Supports." *Urban Institute*, 15 May 2019, https://www.urban.org/urban-wire/middle-income-seniors-face-gap-housing-and-health-supports. Accessed 12 Sept. 2025.
65. "MyLifeSite.net." "Affinity Retirement Communities Give Retirees Access to What They Love." MyLifeSite.net, 2025, https://mylifesite.net/blog/post/affinity-retirement-communities-give-retirees-access-to-what-they-love/.
66. Vaillancourt, Daniel. "Though Still Rare, LGBTQ+ Retirement Communities Rising." AARP, 14 June 2024, https://www.aarp.org/money/retirement/lgbtq-plus-retirement-communities/.
67. Jobera. "Two Income Families Statistics: Insights and Trends ." Jobera, 16 Nov. 2024, jobera.com/two-income-families-statistics/. Accessed 23 Sept. 2025.
68. U.S. Bureau of Labor Statistics. "Comparing Characteristics and Selected Expenditures of Dual- and Single-Income Households with Children." Monthly Labor Review, 11 June 2019, www.bls.gov/opub/mlr/2020/article/comparing-characteristics-and-selected-expenditures-of-dual-and-single-income-households-with-children.htm. Accessed 23 Sept. 2025.
69. "Dual-Earner Family." ScienceDirect Topics, www.sciencedirect.com/topics/psychology/dual-earner-family. Accessed 23 Sept. 2025.

About the Author

Brad Breeding began his career as a personal financial advisor, spending well over a decade serving his clients and earning the prestigious Certified Financial Planner° certification along the way. During this time, he identified a critical need among older adults and their families for impartial support in navigating the complex and financially significant decisions surrounding senior living. This revelation led to the creation of *my*LifeSite, an innovative online platform providing resources, guidance and tools to help people make informed senior living choices- particularly regarding Continuing Care Retirement Communities, also known as "CCRCs" or "Life Plan Communities."

Mr. Breeding's expertise has been sought out by reputable outlets such as Money Magazine, AARP, Kiplinger's, Wall Street Journal's MarketWatch, USA Today, and The New York Times. He also regularly contributes to myLifeSite's blog, adding depth to discussions on aging, wellness, finances, and senior living.

Beyond his writing and media contributions, Mr. Breeding connects with audiences through speaking engagements at senior living and financial advisory conferences, retirement communities, and other forums, where he shares his insights and expertise firsthand. He also contributes to lifelong learning as a volunteer instructor for the Osher Lifelong Learning Institute at respected institutions like Duke University, NC State, and UNC Asheville. This work reflects his dedication to fostering informed senior living and retirement planning decisions.

www.ingramcontent.com/pod-product-compliance
Lightning Source LLC
Chambersburg PA
CBHW060504030426
42337CB00015B/1726